Anti-Inflammatory Diet Cookbook 2020

How to Prevent Degenerative Disease Healing Your Immune System with These Easy Recipes. 21 Days Healthy Meal Plan to Losing Up Pounds Quickly Included.

Table of Contents

Introduction 1
Chapter 1. What is The Anti-Inflammatory Diet? 3
Chapter 2. What Kind of Disease Inflammation Can Cause 8
Chapter 3. Anti-Inflammatory Foods 15
Chapter 4. Benefits of the Anti-Inflammatory Diet 21
Chapter 5. Breakfast and Brunch Recipes 32

    Anti-Inflammatory Cherry Spinach Smoothie 32

    Tropical Carrot Ginger and Turmeric Smoothie 33

    Golden Milk Chia Pudding 34

    No-Bake Turmeric Protein Donuts 35

    Choco-Nana Pancakes 36

    Sweet Potato Cranberry Breakfast bars 37

    Savory Breakfast Pancakes 38

    Scrambled Eggs with Smoked Salmon 39

    Raspberry Grapefruit Smoothie 40

    Breakfast Burgers with Avocado Buns 41

    Spinach Breakfast 42

    Avocado Egg 43

    Healthy Breakfast Chocolate Donuts 44

    Baked Eggs with Portobello Mushrooms 45

    Breakfast Spinach Mushroom Tomato Fry Up 46

    Sweet Cherry Almond Chia Pudding 47

    Pineapple Ginger Smoothie 48

    Beet and Cherry Smoothie 49

    Spicy Pineapple Smoothie 50

    Breakfast Cherry Muffins 51

    Breakfast Shakshuka 52

Anti-Inflammatory Crepes 53

Blueberry Hemp Seed Smoothie 54

Chickpea Scramble with Kale 55

Quick and Creamy Whole Grain Porridge 56

Omega-3 Chocolate Chia Hemp Pudding 57

No Bake Granola Breakfast Bars 58

Anti-Inflammatory Energy Bars 59

No-Bake Chocolate Chia Energy Bars 60

Breakfast Oatmeal Raisin Bars 61

Tropical Chia Seed Oats 62

Quinoa Breakfast Bowl 63

Quinoa Bowls Avocado Egg 64

Anti-Inflammatory Porridge 65

Ginger Turmeric Oatmeal 66

Chapter 6. Main Dishes 67

Quick and Easy Quinoa Orange Salad 67

Herb-Crusted Cauliflower Steaks with Beans and Tomatoes 68

5 Ingredient Thai Pumpkin Soup 70

Mediterranean Tuna Salad 71

Red Lentil and Squash Curry Stew 73

Lemon-Herb Sardine Salad 74

Buddha Bowl with Orange, Kale, Avocado and Wild Rice 75

Kale, Chickpea and Tomato Stew Recipe 77

Smoked Salmon Potato Tartine 78

Kale Caesar Salad with Grilled Chicken Wrap 80

Roasted Red Pepper and Sweet Potato Soup 81

Lettuce Wraps with Smoked Trout 82

Lentil, Beetroot and Hazelnut Salad and a Ginger Dressing 83

Chapter 7. Snacks & Appetizers 84

Spiced Kale Chips 84

Vegetable Nuggets 85
Cabbage Pineapple Slaw 86
Turmeric Muffins 87
Coffee Protein Bars..88
Cauliflower Popcorn..89
Spiced Pumpkin Seeds 90
Curry Roasted Chickpeas..91
Coconut Oats Balls 92
Seasoned Coconut Flakes 93

Chapter 8. Seafood Recipes 94
Poached Halibut and Mushrooms 94
Halibut Stir Fry 95
Steamed Garlic-Dill Halibut 96
Italian Halibut Chowder 97
Pomegranate-Molasses Glazed Salmon 98
Quick Thai Cod Curry 99
Salmon with Sun-Dried Tomatoes and Capers 100
Island Style Sardines 101
Slow Cooked Spanish Cod 102
Multi-Spice Cod Curry.. 103
Poached Cod Asian Style 104
Basil-Avocado Baked Salmon 105
Spicy Baked Cod 106
Cod Casserole Portuguese Style 107
Salmon with Lemon and Dill 108

Chapter 9. Poultry Recipes 109
Herbed Chicken Salad 109
Chicken in Pita Bread 110
Greek Chicken Stew... 111
Easy Stir-Fried Chicken...112

African Chicken Stew 113

Roasted Chicken 115

Turkey Meatballs 116

Chicken Breasts with Stuffing 117

Chicken-Bell Pepper Sauté 118

Avocado-Orange Grilled Chicken 120

Honey Chicken Tagine 121

Brussels Sprouts and Paprika Chicken Thighs 123

Chapter 10. Vegan and Vegetable Recipes 124

Nutty and Fruity Garden Salad 124

Creamy Cauliflower-Broccoli Soup 125

Nutty and Fruity Amaranth Porridge 126

Korean Barbecue Tofu 127

Fruit Bowl with Yogurt Topping 128

Mushroom, Spinach and Turmeric Frittata 129

Roasted Root Vegetables 130

Tropical Fruit Parfait 131

Cinnamon Chips with Avocado-Strawberry Salsa 132

Stir Fried Brussels Sprouts and Carrots 133

Curried Veggies and Poached Eggs 134

Conclusion 136

Introduction

When it comes to any kind of lifestyle shift, it is absolutely necessary to have a plan. Not having a plan can leave you frustrated and broke, especially when it comes to diet. Changing your eating plan affects different parts of your life. You will need to consider your bank account, available time, allergens, your preferences, and the preferences and dietary needs of those in your family - assuming you don't live alone. You will also need to find the types of food to include in your anti-inflammatory diet and which not to. By combining all this information, you can successfully develop a plan that clears your path to decreased inflammation.

The anti-inflammatory benefits come from the synergistic effect of foods consumed together as well as those gotten from individual foods. Even small changes in a person's diet can play a massive role in improving one's health. Therefore, it is vital to focus on goals that are yours and making them as achievable as possible.

For example, eating an extra serving of legumes or fruits at breakfast or lunch is key to helping someone make lasting dietary changes that will help reduce inflammation and enhance overall health. However, based on your past medical history, your diet may need to be modified along with the types of anti-inflammatory foods you should consume. It would be wise to speak with a dietitian before embarking on this journey.

I honestly think there isn't too much thought that needs to be put into starting this diet because it is relatively easy. Just make healthy food choices and find recipes that you might enjoy, because just like any diet, if you don't like it, you will not last very long in it. Please, do remember that you don't have to be 100% perfect. Take it easy, and kiss it. By which I mean Keep It Stupid Simple.

Unless you are under some type of medically specific diet rules, if you're at a friend's wedding, please have a piece of cake. Life is too short, and its meant to be enjoyed. Some people think diets have to be all or nothing which makes them fail to see it through to the end because anything that prevents eating from being a fun activity is considered stressful. So when you're ready to go to the grocery stores, be sure to have a list of healthy whole foods that you would like.

You should try looking for some recipes that seem tasty first. There are thousands online. Also, when you go out to eat, many restaurants make nutritional info available on the menu or sell a lot of whole foods. Feel free to ask restaurants how they prepare foods you're interested in and if need be, request if you would like your item prepared a certain way or with ingredients you want.

Long-term changes take some time to stick, and you need to cut yourself some slack during this process. Don't feel sad if you don't notice any changes over a short period because sustainable lifestyle changes doesn't happen overnight. Rome wasn't built in a day, am I right?

You should also be ready to eliminate the foods that are inflammatory and likely doing your body more harm than good. Also, be prepared because time-consuming preparation is vital, and you will need a lot of preparation time in the kitchen since you will be cooking foods from scratch in a bid to eat nutrient-rich whole foods.

Chapter 1. What is The Anti-Inflammatory Diet?

What I am about to point out might confuse you but stick with me. This will only take a moment, okay?

The Anti-inflammatory diet is not a diet per-se. Its sole purpose is not to promote weight loss, although some people may lose weight during the course of this program. The purpose of this diet is to reduce inflammation by reducing the ingestion of triggers or inflammatory foods. This diet helps individuals to select specific foods that help influence inflammation and enrich the body at the same time.

Did you know that you could incorporate this into your normal recipes? You can do absolutely as you want with it! Except mix it up with inflammatory foods, of course.

The Anti-Inflammatory Diet won't take a lot of trouble to set up seeing as it has only one major rule; no inflammatory foods guys! To set up your personal Anti-Inflammatory Diet, you'll need to know certain things.

•Variety is the spice of life! Get a lot of things in there. Mix it up, make it fun. It doesn't have to taste like cardboard for you to know you're doing it right. Fruits today, veggies tomorrow, that sort of thing.

•Fresh everything! I'm sure we can all agree that everything tastes better fresh. I mean, nobody, absolutely nobody, likes stale bread except my unnecessarily dramatic Hispanic neighbor of course.

•Low or zero consumption of fast food. It's okay to fall off the wagon sometimes but don't do it as often as you'd like. Just ask yourself this one question: cheeseburgers or back pain? Yeah, not so tasty anymore, right?

•Fruits and veggies! I can't emphasize this enough. Fresh fruits and vegetables are absolutely key. Growing up, I never liked vegetables. They were too green and tasted like something I was sure shouldn't be in my mouth. I didn't get why I should be eating grass, but now, there isn't enough GREEN! Some vegetables may not taste or smell very appealing, but the same goes for that wonky knee you have.

Let's Talk Calories

A lot of people might know about calories without actually knowing about calories. I'll explain. A calorie is basically a unit of energy. In regards to food, calories are the amount of energy one can get from food and drinks. Some kinds of food offer more calories than others, while some have zero nutritional value. The amount of calories contained in processed foods is usually written on the wrap or container as most people are completely obsessed with calculating their daily calorie intake.

Food = Calories.

Generally, it's important to keep track or at least know the amount of calories one consumes daily. Calories are very important to one's health; the problem is keeping track of the amount of calories per day. Consumption of foods with a lot of calories regularly leads to obesity while consumption of foods with not enough calories can lead to a person falling beneath the healthy weight range.

Calories are just as important when setting up an Anti-Inflammatory Diet. Without calories, our bodies will fail, and our organs will stop working. No car can run without fuel. The source of the said calories is just as important as the amount of calories themselves. Calories gotten from a large box of pizza is not as healthy as the calories from whole nuts.

Gaining calories is easy. You see, no matter how hard you try to keep proper track of the amount of calories you consume in a day, it's more likely that you will exceed the expected amount. It happens every day to billions of people across the world. You wake up in the morning and make a mental note to consume no more than 2500 calories that day, and somehow, if you calculate properly, you end up consuming 3000 calories.

As I said earlier, calories affect people differently based on physical activities, health, age, sex, and other factors. Best believe a fitness trainer will not be worried about the extra

500 calories because it will be discarded on the treadmill, but the same can't be said for a person using a pacemaker.

Putting on weight is easy. Shedding it however is like trying to remember exactly what you ate when you first turned 3. Okay, maybe that's a bit much, but you get the point.

There are so many effective methods of weight loss, among which are certain Anti-Inflammatory Diet plans, exercise, liposuction, intermittent fasting, etc.

Why is the Anti-Inflammation Diet so important anyway?

Inflammation is the body's immune response that happens when a threat is introduced. So, what are some of the things we ingest that trigger these threats? Doctors and scientists say they include highly processed foods, refined sugars and carbs, and red meats. Alcohol is pretty bad too. Unfortunately, many of the foods incorporated into our diets are processed and highly inflammatory.

So much goodness! So much, yum!

Contrary to popular opinion, it is not just your overall physical health that will benefit from an Anti-Inflammatory Diet. Research from the University of Cambridge also discovered links between inflammatory conditions and mental health, including depression and anxiety. Dr. Golam Khandaker, one of the study's researchers, said: "It's becoming increasingly clear to us that inflammation plays a role in depression and about a third of patients who are resistant to antidepressants show evidence of inflammation."

What to Do?

Successfully switching to an Anti-Inflammatory Diet could be one of the ways to improve your physical and mental health and overall quality of life. It's actually as easy as it sounds... once you get past the fact that you may never eat a pizza again in your life. Haha.

You see, the basic idea behind the anti-inflammatory method of food consumption is quite simple: add nutrients like fiber, vitamins, minerals, good fatty acids, and phytonutrients (plant-based compounds) to your everyday meal, and you reduce inflammation.

Is there a vegan version of the Anti-Inflammatory Diet?

You have a head start if you are already on a diet free of fatty red meat and animal products. The Anti-Inflammatory Diet is easy for vegetarians because the best way to reduce inflammation is to eat a plant-based diet and throw out the meaty stuff. Vegans already do that!

Associate director of nutrition communications at the International Food Information Council Foundation, Ali Webster, Ph.D., RD, speaks of the Anti-Inflammatory Diet as the sort of diet which has nutrient-dense foods rich in antioxidants which help lower inflammation markers in the body. So what kind of foods are we talking about here? Basically, healthy fats, legumes, vegetables, and fruits. Webster also says that red wine is a part of the diet too. I shouldn't have to add that it's good as long as it's in moderation. The foods you can have on the Anti-Inflammatory Diet are strikingly similar to the Mediterranean diet that both terms are used interchangeably.

Mediterranean Diet?

This is the oldest diet in the world, having existed for over three thousand years.

It is mostly in the countries surrounding the Mediterranean sea that we see the religious practice of the Mediterranean diet. Olive trees grow in abundance in this region; fruits are usually in season during the four seasons due to their mild climate and seafood is a major part of the diet thanks to the fact that fishing is one of the main occupations there. Also, the herbs in this region are not only used for cooking but also medicinal purposes.

Many institutions depict the Mediterranean diet food components in a pyramid format. They came up with the Mediterranean diet inverted (upside-down) food pyramid that emphasizes on food items that should be eaten more, like fruits, vegetables, olive oil and fish, and food that should be eaten less like animal products, dairy products, and meat. Items at the bottom of the pyramid are very essential for healthy eating, and these should form 75% of your meals while items towards the tip of the pyramid are not so important and should be taken in moderation.

Why should I get on a Mediterranean diet?

•Great health... Duh!The Mediterranean diet plan shows exactly how much a specific food item should be eaten as it should promote good health by consuming only healthy food and hitting the gym every now and then. This means eating more vegetables and fruits instead of processed foods. It doesn't tell us to totally bag and trash the sweets and fatty foods but to take it down a lot of notches

•Meat is not your best friend.At the base of the pyramid, you can see that meat is the only item shown to be eaten at least once a month. Now, this shouldn't shock you at all since most kinds of meat, especially the ones that contain fats, make us feel a bit wonky. The unsaturated fats that it gives off with absolutely no tax or charge are the main source of bad cholesterol, which also triggers various ailments.

•More nutritional value.Foods that are recommended to be eaten in moderation are those found on the mid-part of the pyramid. These are usually composed of animal products and fish. You'll also notice that pastries, legumes, vegetables, and fruits are situated at the bottom part. These are the foods that should be eaten daily due to the high amount of nutritional value. Your body will thank you, I promise.

•No more laziness and tiredness! This is why the Mediterranean diet food pyramid specifically tells us to eat light foods, thereby reducing the fat intake and giving us more energy when we want to do stuff like, lift a bus.

•Good fats only. There are two classes of fats, the good fats, and bad fats. The pyramid says it's okay to consume olive oil which is regarded as the good fat. This oil is usually found in some vegetable salads. It doesn't present any risks since it promotes good health as it helps in lowering the bad cholesterol in our bodies.

Chapter 2. What Kind of Disease Inflammation Can Cause

If we make a comparison, we would soon see that most of the causes of Inflammation are related to diet, so we are keeping this at the top of the list. Harmful substances such as refined fats, animal products, and refined carbohydrates cause damage in the long run. It should be noted though that carbohydrates do not directly contribute to inflammation, refined foods with higher concentration and fats are found to be naturally dense with inflammation-causing substances that affect the gut and increases inflammation.

The types of fat consumed by an individual also play a role here. Back in the early days, when everything was simple, people used to stay on a diet that was well-balanced on both Omega-3 and Omega-6 fats. However, modern diets tend to have a high concentration of Omega-6 fat as opposed to Omega-3 fat; this increases the possibility of suffering from inflammation by 10-20%. It is important for the body to have a good supply of Omega-3 fatty acids because the Omega-6 and Omega-3, both compete for the same COX enzymes, which are needed to build large fatty molecules.

COX-2 enzyme, in particular, is essential for making inflammatory prostaglandins. Too much Omega-6 fatty acids will result in the domination of this enzyme, and the body will not be able to utilize the enzyme anymore in conjunction with Omega-3 fats to reduce inflammation. Nowadays, fats are chemically modified, and this plays a greater role in inflammation as well.

They are made to be more inexpensive, which results in the production of highly inflammatory products. Aging The natural process of aging contributes to inflammation, as well. As we age, the body's cells can regenerate, but most of them start to die, leaving behind waste material that can trigger inflammation.

Obesity and Inactivity Excessive inactivity can and will often lead to obesity, which is a major cause of inflammation. Adipose tissue, the layer of fat that is found right under our skin, is actually responsible for much more than just keeping it warm. It is a metabolically active layer that causes the body to change the body chemistry and is also affected by the body's other systems.

The fat layer contains a large number of white blood cells and a greater level of fat. The cell count is linked together. Meaning, the more fat there is, the greater the number of white cells will be present. These cells often release pro-inflammatory substances that gradually contribute to the rise of inflammatory effects. Sleep Deprivation Researchers have shown that a lack of sleep is linked to the formation of certain infection-fighting white blood cells such as T-Cells.

Depriving ourselves of sleep will cause the number of T-Cells to decrease, which in turn increases the number of inflammation-promoting cytokines. Stress Cortisol is a hormone produced by adrenal glands and used to manage the body's response to stress. It helps stimulate bursts of energy and suppresses pro-inflammatory substances.

This also helps to reduce stress by counteracting the effects of pro-inflammatory eicosanoids. However, if you stress too much, the amount of cortisol might increase to a dramatic level that will cause your immune cells to lose sensitivity to this hormone and trigger inflammation. Sun Exposure This might seem a little bit surprising, but excessive exposure to sunlight can often result in an individual suffering from inflammation. Sunburn or over-exposure encourages the formation of free radicals under the skin surface. Just to let you know, free radicals are unstable molecules that tend to destroy injury-fighting cells and lower the number of white blood cells present in the body. As you may have guessed, this lowers the strength of the body's immune system and leads to inflammatory attacks.

Smoking Exposure to various toxins such as cigarette smoke plays a high role in inflammation. Either second hand or first hand, inhaled tobacco tends to cripple the body's capacity to fight diseases by suppressing the production of white blood cells. Craze Behind Inflammation So, why are people heading for an anti-inflammatory diet? Despite having the best technology and health care services in the world, America is still suffering from an epidemic of chronic inflammation and other chronic inflammatory diseases.

The change in the form of a modern diet is contributing to increasing the number of incidents as well. When we are referring to chronic inflammation, we are implying various diseases such as arthritis, asthma among the long-term illnesses/diseases. As stated at the beginning of the chapter, In the US alone, nearly 43 million people suffer from arthritis, and 25 million suffer from Asthma.

Those are no small numbers, and the need for Americans to find a proper solution for the anti-inflammatory regime is at an all-time high. Science of Inflammation Now that you have a little idea of just how severe of a problem inflammation is, let us have a look at how inflammation works, and what happens to your body during inflammation. When your body needs to respond to an injury, it tends to mobilize an army of specialized cells to fend of the invading organism and toxins. These cells prepare pathways for fighter cells to attack and completely engulf the attackers.

Once that has happened, another group of cells tends to signal to the body and let it know the fighter cells have accomplished their task, and the body is allowed to stop the production of preparatory and fighter cells. These result in a sort of cleanup that clears up the leftover fighter cells from the battlefield and repairs any damage. Simply put, there are two steps to this response: pro-inflammatory and anti-inflammatory. Each cell involved in the pro stage builds on the work of the previous cells and helps to make the immune reaction stronger for any upcoming attack. During the pro period, symptoms such as redness, swelling, itching are common. The anti-inflammatory is the reverse of pro-inflammatory, and it works to lower the effects of inflammation.

A variety of substances used to block inflammation are made from essential fatty acids, which the body isn't able to produce on its own. These acids must be obtained through supplements or foods.

Two essential ones are Omega-3 and Omega-6. Omega-6 tends to increase inflammation, while Omega-3 helps to reduce it. It should be noted that what I wrote above is a simplified version of the whole mechanism, and there is a lot more to it. There are various substances that play a deeper role in the whole infrastructure that allows the body to control its inflammatory mechanism. Some of the crucial ones are Histamine: White blood cells near an injury tend to release a substance known as histamine. They increase the permeability of blood vessels around the wound that signals fighter cells and other substances to regulate immune response and come to the sight of injury.

Histamine also causes redness and swelling around the affected region and causes runny nose, rash, itchy eyes. Cytokines: These are proteins that are activated by pro-inflammatory eicosanoids to signal fighter cells to gather at the injury site. They are responsible for diverting energy from the body to catalyst the healing process. The release of these substances tends to cause tiredness and decrease appetite. C-Reactive Protein: Cytokines alongside other pro-inflammatory eicosanoids are closely involved in the activation of a substance known as C-Reactive Protein.

This particular organic compound produced by the liver responds to messages that are sent out by white blood cells. The C-Reactive proteins tend to bind the site of injury and act as a sort of surveillance unit that helps to identify the invading bodies. Leukocytes: Several types of leukocytes (also known as white blood cells) are critical to the process of neutralizing invading substances. Neutrophils, for example, are small, agile and are able to first arrive at the scene of the crime to ingest small microbes.

However, large substances such as macrophages as required to tackle a large number of microbes. There are a few more, but the gist still remains the same. When your body starts to suffer from an uncontrolled inflammation attack, the action of these and similar substances tend to get out of control, which results in extremely uncomfortable situations.

Harmful side effects of Inflammation Uncontrolled inflammation results in diseases that are known as autoimmune diseases. While there are a large number of them out there, some of the more prominent ones are Type 1 Diabetes: Type 1 Diabetes can cause the immune system to attack and destroy insulin-producing cells in your pancreas that disrupt the regulation of sugar levels in your body. Rheumatoid Arthritis: RA causes the immune system to attack certain joints that can result in discomfort and pain. Psoriatic

Arthritis: This causes skin cells to multiply rapidly, which results in red and scaly patches on your skin called plaques. Multiple Sclerosis: MS tends to damage the protective coating that surrounds nerve cells (known as myelin sheath) and affects the transmission of neural messages between the brain and body. This leads to weakness, balance issues, along with other symptoms. Inflammatory Bowel Syndromes: This disease causes irritation of the intestinal lining. Graves' Disease: This disease attacks the thyroid gland in your neck and causes it to overproduce hormones, which results in an imbalance. Cancer: Cancerous tumors tend to secret substances that attract cytokines and free radicals that cause inflammation, which can lead to tumors growing.

If you already suffer from inflammation, it could make the situation words. Alzheimer's: The brain does not have pain receptors, but that doesn't mean it will not be able to feel the effects of inflammation. Researchers have recently discovered that people with a high level of Omega-6 fatty acids tend to have a greater chance of developing Alzheimer's. Different symptoms of Inflammation While there are different types of diseases that are caused by Inflammation, the early symptoms of them are similar. These include: Fatigue Muscle ache Low-grade fever Redness and swelling Numbness in your feet and hands Loss of hair Skin rash These are often accompanied by the symptoms that are specific to any disease the patient might be suffering from.

About Anti-Inflammatory Diet, generally speaking, an anti-inflammatory diet consists of a diet comprised of foods targeted towards the reduction of the uncontrolled inflammatory response in the body. The anti-inflammatory diet is rich in foods packed with anti-oxidants that are reactive molecules in the food to help to reduce free radicals, which causes cell damage to the body. There are many popular diets already following the anti-inflammatory principle, such as the Mediterranean diet, which is comprised of fish, good fats, and whole grains.

Great Tips for Anti-Inflammatory Success

Even if you are following a completely anti-inflammatory diet, the following steps will help you to further up the ante and improve your condition: Eat a wide variety of fruits and vegetables of different colors. Reduce the amount of junk food you consume. Eliminate sugary beverages and sodas from your diet. Create healthy shopping lists; avoids buying unhealthy items. Carry anti-inflammatory snacks while you are on the road. Drink water. Maintain a healthy calorie intake. Try including Omega-3 supplements and turmeric in your diet. Exercise on a regular basis. Make sure to get proper sleep. These will help you to accelerate your progress significantly

Foods Good for Anti-Inflammatory Diet

Despite popular belief, following an anti-inflammatory diet, isn't challenging. The following foods will encourage a healthy anti-inflammatory lifestyle: dark leafy greens such as kale and spinach blueberries, cherries, blackberries dark red grapes cauliflower and broccoli green tea beans and lentils red wine (in moderation) avocado and coconut olives extra virgin olive oil walnuts, almonds, pistachio, pine nuts coldwater fish; salmon and sardines spices and herbs; cinnamon , turmeric dark chocolate watermelon onion whole grains; brown rice, bulgur, quinoa eggs tomatoes.

These are just the basics; there is a lot more to look out for.

Foods Bad for Anti-Inflammatory Diet Foods you should avoid if you want to keep your inflammation in check. Sugary foods; soda, baked sweets, candy, sweetened coffee Vegetable oil products; mayonnaise, BBQ sauce, potato chips, crackers Fried foods; French fries, fish sticks, fried chicken, onion rings Refined flour products; pizza, pasta, flour tortillas, bagels, crackers Dairy; milk, yogurt, butter, soft cheeses Artificial sweeteners; means no-sugar-added products such as diet coke Artificial additives; including breakfast cereals, ice cream, candy Saturated fats; burgers, chips, pizza, and candy Conventional grain-fed meats; beef, pork, chicken Processed meats; bacon, sausage, jerky, hot dogs Gluten from store-bought products; bread, white flour Alcohol in excess Trans food fats; margarine, baked goods such as cookies, doughnuts, muffins Fast food.

Frequently Asked Questions 1. Should I Detox Before Anti-Inflammation? When you are detoxing your body, you are essentially flushing out the harmful toxins that have accumulated in your body. Completing a detox before embarking on your anti-inflammation is an excellent way of ensuring the effectiveness of your new lifestyle.

2. Should I See A Doctor for My Inflammation? An anti-inflammation lifestyle is a regime largely based on vegetables and requires an individual to omit certain products such as dairy products and red meat. If you are already following a similar kind of diet, such as vegan, then you would have fewer issues changing your eating habits. However, if you are taking such a step for the first time and trying to completely shift your lifestyle, it is recommended you consult a physician to ascertain you are in a healthy place to change your eating habits. Alternatively, if you are already suffering from an auto-immune disease, then it is even more advisable to consult with your doctor in order to create a meal plan according to your requirements.

3. Should I Exercise More? Having a fit and healthy body definitely helps reduce the possibility of experiencing issues when you begin this new lifestyle. If you are obese, you may face some inflammatory reactions, so it is better to start with a minimum level of exercise in your day-to-day routine before progressing to more strenuous exercising.

Chapter 3. Anti-Inflammatory Foods

There are numerous foods that can help tackle inflammation. This chapter will cover most popular foods, which have anti-inflammatory properties, their active ingredients and the method in which they work.

An inflammatory response is caused by the activation of white blood cells in response to foreign entities in the body.

Whenever a molecule enters our bloodstream, our white blood cells immediately start to recognize that molecule as either belonging to the body or alien. If the molecule is foreign, it is tagged and removed to prevent it from causing any harm. The white blood cells also cause a series of processes, which are intended to minimize damage and contain pathogens.

For example, the chemicals released by the white blood cells often cause fluid to flow into the affected areas, therefore causing swelling. Likewise, redness often occurs due to increased blood flow (this helps white blood cells move to the appropriate place).

It is important to note that inflammation doesn't just affect the skin and joints, but it can also affect the internal organs. As you might expect, inflammation of the internal organs can cause serious health problems. Inflammation of the heart, for example, is called myocarditis and is associated with shortness of breath. Conversely, inflammation of the kidneys is also associated with high blood pressure and even outright kidney failure.

In some circumstances the inflammatory response arises due to a false positive, such as particular allergens, arthritis or an excessive intake of certain foods.

Inflammation is associated with redness, swollen warm joints, joint pain or stiffness and overall lack of malleability in the joints.

Inflammation has also been connected with a general reduction in well-being due to a myriad of flu-like symptoms such as pain, fatigue, headaches, fever and loss of appetite.

Therefore, if you find yourself suffering from any of these inflammatory symptoms then it can be useful to incorporate anti-inflammatory foods into your diet.

Current understanding is that there are dozens of potential sources of inflammation and just as many molecules that can help mediate both the causes and symptoms.

In particular, food scientists often record the presence of two proteins in the bloodstream (C-reactive protein & interluekin-6) as accurate indicators of the level of inflammation people suffer.

These two proteins are known to be controlled by omega-3 fatty acids, which are also known to have several other benefits (such as improving cognition).

Omega-3 fatty acids are present in several types of fish, including but not limited to

Salmon

Sardines

Tuna

Anchovies

Additionally, numerous nuts have omega-3, especially walnuts and almonds.

Inflammation is also thought to be reduced by a stronger and more efficient immune system. The exact mechanism by which a better immune system alleviates inflammatory response is not known, although there are a few hypotheses.

Namely, it is thought, that a more efficient immune system may manage problems faster, resulting in less time spent in an inflammatory response. Alternatively, a more productive immune system might produce fewer 'false positives' and react less severely to molecules, which are not genuinely harmful.

Regardless of the method, there is therefore reason to believe in a link between molecules that support the immune system (such as anti-oxidants) and lower levels of inflammation. The foods highest in anti-oxidants tend to be herbs & spices, although there are exceptions.

In particular the following foods are known to be especially potent;

Cloves

Ginger

Rosemary

Turmeric

Cinnamon

Allspice

Marjoram

Sage

Thyme

Italian Spice

Although you can supplement your meals with herbs and spices, their effect will be limited due to the small amount actually consumed. Therefore it is also important to incorporate other foods, which are less powerful but can be eaten in greater quantities.

Many fruits & vegetables contain also contain high amounts of antioxidants and they can also feasibly be eaten in more meaningful quantities. Strong antioxidant choices include blueberries, blackberries, cherries, strawberries, spinach, kale & broccoli.

Additionally, foods high in monounsaturated fat should also be included in an anti-inflammatory diet. The exact reason why monounsaturated fat seems to have an anti-inflammatory effect is not known, although it has been suggested to be partially due to the presence of antioxidants and partially due to how monounsaturated fat promotes the absorption of vitamins & minerals (promoting overall bodily health).

Foods high in monosatured fat include nuts, seeds, olives, avocados and some types of vegetable oils. In particular, walnuts & almonds should make particularly prominent choices due to the fact that they also contain omega-3 and omega-6 fatty acids, which as previously mentioned, also have anti-inflammatory properties.

Other anti-inflammatory foods include most types of beans (such as kidney beans or butter beans). Beans are low in the glycaemic index, which categorizes foods by how quickly the carbohydrates within them are absorbed.

It is widely believed that inflammation may be partially due to excessive sugar and carbohydrate intake, foods with low glycaemic index values arguably have anti-inflammatory properties too.

Likewise, beans are high in fibre, which may promote overall gastrointestinal health and reduce intestinal inflammation. Fibre also lowers levels of the previously before-mentioned C-reactive protein (or CRP for short).

As a general rule of thumb, colorful fruits and vegetables are typically associated with both high levels of anti-oxidants as well as high levels of fibre, making them fantastic at lowering inflammation.

Moreover, several types of red wine can also be considered to be anti-inflammatory. Red wine, especially red wine originating from the Mediterranean and France, has been noted for its high levels of anti-oxidants.4

However, red wine also contains a molecule called Resveratrol, which is under research for its anti-inflammatory properties. With this being said, keeping alcohol intake within a reasonable level is obviously important for overall health.

Additionally, leafy greens (such as spinach, kale, collard greens & Swiss chard) are rich in multiple types of molecules that reduce inflammation.

Finally, consider adding tea (such as matcha tea & tulsi tea), blueberries, fermented foods, shiitake mushrooms & garlic.

To add to all of this, you might want to consider cutting some foods from your diet. Many of the usual unhealthy foods are suspected to increase inflammatory symptoms, such as processed foods, foods high in unhealthy fats and sodium.

Nonetheless, there are also some offenders you might not expect. The so-called nightshade branch of foods (which includes eggplant, tomatoes, peppers &) has been accused of exacerbating inflammation and arthritis. However, actual scientific support for this claim is rather sketchy.

To conclude, an anti-inflammatory diet would consist of a diet centred on the following foods;

Herbs & Spices

Fish

Nuts, Seeds, Avocado & Vegetable Oil

Fruit & Vegetables

Beans

Red Wine

Leafy Greens

The remainder of this eBook will provide you with numerous recipes high in these anti-inflammatory foods.

Chapter 4. Benefits of the Anti-Inflammatory Diet

The anti-inflammatory diet has a lot of health benefits. Surprisingly, it has similar benefits to the top leading diet out there. Make sure you read them, allowing you to understand how this diet can help you in the long run. One thing we want you to keep in mind would be that many users might notice different results from this diet. Many users claim benefits that are not even listed here since they are not so common. The anti-inflammatory diet is truly a surprise when it comes to delivering the results; this diet works very differently on everyone else.

Make sure that you understand that you will see benefits that are not common, most likely. However, you will see the basic benefits of this diet, regardless of who you are. I would also like to point out that these benefits are from personal experience only, even though some have been backed up by science that does not mean all of them are. You see, the health and fitness industry is so personal that getting an accurate understanding of what a certain diet could do is very much impossible. All we can do is understand the studies which have been done by scientist and try and relate it to us, which is all we can do in terms of getting to understand what the anti-inflammatory diet can offer us in terms of health benefits. We will list out all of the most common benefits associated with this diet, but please keep in mind that you might see different results from this diet and that it can be quite different from what you expected. None the less, this is one diet you have to test out for yourself.

Weight-Loss

As you know, there are many ways to lose weight. However, one of the most popular methods being used to lose weight is the anti-inflammatory diet, and there is a good reason behind it. Many people do not know this, but the anti-inflammatory diet is perhaps the best way for someone to lose "body fat" instead of "body-weight." When following most diets, followers tend to lose a ton of weight, but most of the time, it is muscle and water weight they are getting rid of.

On the other hand, the anti-inflammatory diet makes you lose more body fat. Here is how it works, when you are eating right healthy foods for a prolonged period, you have burned out all your glycogen stores as your caloric intake drops. Which makes the body hit your reserves, and that, of course, is your body fat. You will be burning more body fat instead of muscle mass or glycogen, which makes it ideal for people looking to lose weight. Also, as you know, proper diet plays a huge role in affecting your hormones. Your insulin will flatline, and your growth hormone will go up, this will prime your body to burn body fat instead and will do so in a healthy manner.

Increased Longevity

There have been many studies showings that the anti-inflammatory diet can boost endurance. As you might know by now that anti-inflammatory diet can help you with cell rejuvenation or also known as autophagy, this process enables you to get rid of the old and weak cells and replace it with newer, stronger ones. This process has shown to increase longevity and overall well-being, which is one of the reasons why the anti-inflammatory diet can help you live a longer life. Moreover, some studies are showing that reducing calories in animals by 30% to 40% has shown to increase their lifespan. However, there is no study done on humans claiming such. Nonetheless, some studies are suggesting that monkeys that ate less food but more on the anti-inflammatory side lived longer. However, there was another study indicating that it wasn't the case on 25-year-old long research done by another party.

Although there is no actual study backing these claims up, it does show that people who ate less had fewer risks of diseases, which could lead to longevity. Which is excellent news when looking at it from that angle, there is a lot of disease prevention that comes with the anti-inflammatory diet, but we will talk about those later in this chapter. However, the main thing to remember would be the fact that an anti-inflammatory diet helps with autophagy, which enables you to rejuvenate cells, which makes it very evident that the anti-inflammatory diet can help you with longevity and overall well-being, which is a great thing to consider.

Prevent Diseases

There are many diseases present in today's day and age, and it very common to meet someone suffering from one. The anti-inflammatory diet has shown to lower the risk of many diseases, and we will be discussing all the disorders the anti-inflammatory diet can help get rid of. One of the many conditions anti-inflammatory diet could help manage would be Alzheimer's and Parkinson's.

As you know, the anti-inflammatory diet helps boost brain health and to lower the risk of neurologic diseases. Some studies are showing that the anti-inflammatory diet can help reduce the risk of depression, even though some people might not consider this a condition, it is still a significant issue in our society. The anti-inflammatory diet has also shown to reduce cholesterol. A 2010 study on overweight women found that the anti-inflammatory diet improved hosts of health complications, including cholesterol levels (LDL) and blood pressure, which is also known as the silent killer.

The anti-inflammatory diet also helps with reducing type 2 diabetes, and there was one study done on men, which showed that anti-inflammatory helped them stop insulin treatment. Although we do not recommend you try this if you have type 2 diabetes, that goes to show you the power of the diet and insulin resistance.

Nonetheless, many studies are suggesting that the anti-inflammatory diet can lower the risk of diabetes. Another devastating disease in which an anti-inflammatory diet helps getting rid of would be cancer. As you know, the anti-inflammatory diet enables you to have a less hospitable environment for the cancer cells, which makes this diet an excellent idea for people who are looking to reduce this risk.

In regards to a healthier life, the anti-inflammatory diet has also shown to reduce the risk of obesity. One study done on obese women suggested that an anti-inflammatory diet reduced the risk of obesity in women, which makes sense as it helps you lose and manage body weight.

These facts about the anti-inflammatory diet show you how the anti-inflammatory diet can help you get free of many diseases, and some have been backed up with detailed studies, whereas others are still being researched.

Nonetheless, you can't say that about other diets out there. The anti-inflammatory diet will help you to get rid of many things and prevent you from further having any diseases. There is no better way of getting rid of illness or problems without the use of modern medicine, and this diet is so powerful that it will also boost your immune system, which will help you avoid small issues like the common flu. All in all, there are many rejuvenating properties that come along with the anti-inflammatory diet, so do not overlook it and keep all the positives in mind before you look at the negatives.

Reduce Stress and Inflammation

The anti-inflammatory diet has shown a significant reduction in inflammation. As you know, inflammation causes many chronic diseases such as Alzheimer's, dementia, obesity, diabetes, and much more. Now, there are many ways that the anti-inflammatory diet helps you get rid of inflammation. The first one being autophagy, as you know, anti-inflammatory diet helps you with cell rejuvenation cleans up itself by eating out the old self and rejuvenating them with the newer, stronger ones. If your body does not regenerate itself with more new cells, the older ones that have stayed for an extended period can cause inflammation.

Now that we've talked about many ways. An anti-inflammatory diet enables you to reduce inflammation; let us talk about how the anti-inflammatory diet can help you get rid of stress. You see, inflammation and stress go hand in hand. If you have high levels of inflammation, chances are your stress levels are going to be higher. This means that if you lower your inflammation, you will reduce your stress levels, and as you know, this diet helps with better brain function. An anti-inflammatory diet enables you to send better signals to your brain, which would equal a better functioning brain.

When your mind is functioning at its absolute peak, your levels of stress dropdown. Better brain function will also help you get rid of any stress you might be having and will give you overall better health can help you reduce weight. Overall, the health benefits you get from the anti-inflammatory diet will help you get rid of your stress or at least lower it. This means, even if you are not facing any stress-related issues, the anti-inflammatory diet will help you have a better functioning brain and also help you get rid of any mental fog or stress you might be dealing with. With that in mind, always make sure you consult a physician if you are noticing much more stress than you can handle, as it can be something severe and not fixable by the anti-inflammatory diet.

Body Detox and Cell Cleaned

Detoxing your body is very important when it comes to living a long healthy life; many people detox their body through juice cleanse or other methods out there when the truth is that they do not work. Time and time again, the anti-inflammatory diet has shown to help detox your body at both the cellular level and digestive level, which means the anti-inflammatory diet is a lot more superior when it comes to cleaning your body.

As you know, from a cellular level anti-inflammatory diet detoxifies your body with the process of autophagy, what this process does it eat out the bad cells and replace it with healthier and much more stronger cells. Through this process, you will notice benefits such as a stronger immune system, prevention of diseases, and insulin sensitivity. It has also shown to reduce the risk of cancer, which is a great thing to know. Overall, this is how the anti-inflammatory diet detoxifies your body from a cellular level. Let us talk about how the anti-inflammatory diet helps you detoxify from a digestive level standpoint.

People say that your gut is your second brain, and studies are showing how your stomach and mind are connected. This means if your digestive system isn't functioning at its absolute peak, then chances are your brain will not either. It is essential to have your gut clean and working correctly, and this diet helps a lot with this process.

It has been shown that the anti-inflammatory diet can help you clean out your gut and intestines, getting rid of debris and junk. Sometimes, it is essential that we give your digestive system a break from eating all those "bad foods" regularly. Once you start your diet, your body will begin to slowly get rid of all the toxins present in your gut, and you see when you are eating all the junk food, your body doesn't get a chance to clean itself.

Your body has to focus on digesting the food instead of cleaning out the toxins when you give your body a break from eating. It will start to clean out its gut, which makes this process great for people who have a lot of cleaning to do, but it will help you digest your food a lot better and also think better. The detoxifying body helps you tremendously with lowering the risk of diseases, which will help you live a longer life.

By now, you can see the pattern; an anti-inflammatory diet helps you from every single place to prevent diseases and many other complications. Which means there are more positives than negatives with the anti-inflammatory diet, as we go along in this chapter, you will learn more benefits when it comes to an anti-inflammatory diet. However, remember that these will only work unless you do. You have to follow the anti-inflammatory diet the right way to see these benefits. With that being said, I hope you have learned a lot from this book as we are just getting started. Now let us move on to another benefit.

Improved Insulin Sensitivity

As you know, the anti-inflammatory diet helps you get more insulin sensitive, which allows you with many things. To understand it better, let me explain to you how insulin works. Every time you eat a meal, your insulin spikes up, then insulin is used to shuttle food either to muscle or your fat store.

When you have too much glycogen in your bloodstream, your body will send that energy to your fat stores. Whereas if you're insulin sensitive, your body will send the glycogen to muscle stores and will be used for energy. When you are insulin sensitive, you are more likely to use up all the glycogen from your food faster, and not requiring your glycogen to be converted into fats.

How anti-inflammatory diet helps with curing insulin resistance is by using up all the glycogen stores, making your body use up fat stores and when you eat good food, it will use up all the glycogen and shuttle it straight to the muscle mass to be used for energy instead of being stored into fat. That is how the anti-inflammatory diet helps you become more insulin sensitive; the benefits of being insulin sensitive are many. Once you become insulin sensitive, you will notice more mental energy and less mental fog, and you will also see less fat being stored in your body, which makes it ideal for people looking to lose fat and or gain muscle.

Being insulin sensitive will also help you gain more muscle since most of the energy will be sent out to your muscle stores. It will be used to build stronger muscles instead of storing it into fat. Being insulin sensitive is a must, as it will also help you get rid of possible diseases such as type 2 diabetes. All in all, the anti-inflammatory diet helps you tremendously with insulin sensitively, which will overall help you live a healthier life.

Increased Production of Neurotrophic Growth Factor

Believe it or not, the anti-inflammatory diet affects your brain in a significant way. It all happens from the help of brain-derived neurotrophic growth factor, also known as (BDNF), this helps promote neuroplasticity. Neuroplasticity is your brain's ability to migrate and shapeshift, and this helps our brain to produce new brain cells. Once you have an ample supply of BDNF, we can preserve older cells while producing new brain cells. This means your brain will be healthy and will keep growing because of the new cells coming. Multiple studies are showing that anti-inflammatory diet to improve brain-derived neurotrophic growth factor, more specifically when it has to do with synapses, this is where your neurotransmitter travel cell to cell.

Diet has shown to promote this, and there was a study done where it showed diet following the 80/20 rule has shown to increase levels of brain-derived neurotrophic growth factor by around 50-400%. Now we know that diet helps promote (BDNF), more explicitly, diet helps when it comes down to synapses. It improves what is known as synaptic plasticity, and this helps modulate our moods better. For instance, we can strengthen a synapse or weaken a synapse. This process enables you to be in the moment when you need to be happy or scared; this will help you modulate that accordingly.

In layman's term, this process helps us change our mood and be reactive at the moment. For example, if you need to be more focused, you will be able to because you are modulating it. When your brain-derived neurotrophic growth factor increases, so do your (BDNF) expression. This process helps you produce more brain cells and protect more brain cells, and this affects your cells at a genetic level altering our DNA. Which makes diet one of the best ways to protect your brain, and this gives your mind all the help it needs to preserve and recycle out old cells.

Another thing which it helps with is producing more growth hormone, and there was a study done where it showed upwards of a 4000% increase in growth hormone levels. Which is huge when it comes to improvements, as you know, growth hormone is responsible for many things of them being weight loss. It is a plus to have higher amounts of growth hormone in both men and women. I know that the information was very scientific, so to put in straightforward terms, your brain will rejuvenate a lot quicker.

It will also help you with controlling your moods, which will make it easy to adapt at the moment. Brain-derived neurotrophic growth factors will also help you produce higher levels of growth hormone and serotonin, which are both crucial for mental well-being. For readers looking for mental clarity and fewer mood swings throughout the day, an anti-inflammatory diet is your answer to all.

Boost Immune System

There is a reason why having a healthy immune system is fundamental, as it will help you get less sick and be more "immune" to disease. The anti-inflammatory diet has shown to increase the immune system, so we will talk about how it boosts the immune system. There was a study done on stem cells when it comes down to a diet individual; more specifically, they took a look at how the stem cells rejuvenated.

The study concluded that anti-inflammatory diet depleted white blood cells, which is precisely what we want so our body can produce better and more efficient cells, which lead to more production of stem cells and lesser of white cells. Once you start to get rid of your old white blood cells, you will begin to produce new ones, which will overall help you recover faster. This study also found that there was a reduced amount of protein kinase A (PKA), which allows the stem cells to regenerate. If you have a lower amount of (PKA), this means that it will enable the cells to turn on the regeneration mode, which will allow them to create new cells.

As you know, the anti-inflammatory diet has shown to reduce insulin levels, which is a great thing for someone looking to boost their immune system. There was a study done showing that high amounts of insulin levels, prevented "T" cells from doing its job effectively. The "T" cells are here to suppress inflammation, and to fight off illness, "T" cells are most of the time responsible for getting rid of toxins, which cause disease and inflammation. When your insulin levels are high, "T" cells are not performing at their highest potential, which causes our immune system to drop down.

When you are diet, there isn't a requirement for insulin spikes, which lets our body help the "T" cells work at a higher level and, overall, boosting our immune system. Since you aren't eating foods that will spike your insulin a crazy amount, this will give your digestive system and organs a break. When you eat a big meal, around 70% of the blood and energy goes to your stomach to digest it. This means when you are on a diet, you give your body a chance to recover. Everything is healing when you are on the anti-inflammatory diet, which includes the digestive system. Meaning, your gut will be working a lot more effectively once you have given it some time to heal.

As you know, digestion plays a significant role in both our mental health and immune system, about 60% of our immune system is in our colon, which means when you are the diet, you are recovering your whole body and overall boosting your immune system. You will be doing yourself an excellent service if you can manage to boost your immune system, and with all the backed-up science showing how anti-inflammatory diet can help you promote your immune system and reduce many other health problems, there is no reason not to start the anti-inflammatory diet as soon as possible.

More Energy and Muscle Mass Increased

Even if your goal isn't to put on more muscle, it is still good to have more muscle mass as it helps you with many things. However, the main thing having higher amounts of muscle mass helps you with would be a fat loss; having a higher muscle mass will help you burn more fat since it increases your metabolic rate. Do not worry, and you do not have to look like a bodybuilder for that to happen; nonetheless, it is essential to have the right amount of muscle mass, especially for women.

The anti-inflammatory diet has shown to increase and preserve muscle mass, so let us talk about how that happens. There was a study done between two groups of men, one followed an 80/20 diet method, and the other followed a healthy eating pattern. Both groups followed the same workout but a different diet, one group which supported the 80/20 diet, which we will talk about later in this book, they noticed after eight weeks was, both the groups gained and preserved the same amount of muscle, but the group who were following the anti-inflammatory diet lost more fat.

This shows that the anti-inflammatory diet not only helped followers gain muscle and preserve it, but it also helped them lose fat simultaneously. The main reason behind that is growth hormone, as you know, the anti-inflammatory diet has shown to increase growth hormone in our bodies. What growth hormone mainly does, it allows a lot less muscle breakdown and to burn more fat, which is one of the main reasons why the anti-inflammatory diet is so beneficial for building and preserving muscle mass.

Another great benefit of the anti-inflammatory diet, as you know, is higher energy levels, and there is a reason behind it. Many people know how it feels to have a sugar crash, you feel tired and lethargic, and the culprit behind it is insulin. When insulin is spiked up, your energy level goes down as this gives your brain a signal to relax. When you are an anti-inflammatory diet, there are no insulin spikes throughout the day, which provides you with more energy.

Another reason why you have more energy when you are diet is that your body goes into a fight or flight response and since your body is eating food it was intended to eat in the first place, and our body produces more adrenaline throughout the day, which gives you more energy as you go along. Just be aware, at the beginning of your diet journey, you might feel less energized.

The reason behind it is because your body is still getting used to these changes, but after a week or two, you should start to notice more energy. Use the power to get more work done at work and gym. In my opinion, and this is the most significant benefit which comes along with the anti-inflammatory diet. More energy makes you feel a lot better when you are looking towards making it through those long days.

These are all the main benefits that come along when you start the diet, and the benefits genuinely outweigh all the negatives which might happen. These benefits can be life-changing to most people, lowering the risk of diseases and increasing longevity it's a fantastic thing to have. anti-inflammatory diet provides you with that and then some.

Chapter 5. Breakfast and Brunch Recipes

Anti-Inflammatory Cherry Spinach Smoothie

Preparation time: 5 minutes

Cooking time: 0 minutes

Servings: 1

Ingredients:

1 cup plain kefir

1 cup frozen cherries, pitted

½ cup baby spinach leaves

¼ cup mashed ripe avocado

1 tablespoon almond butter

1-piece peeled ginger (1/2 inch)

1 teaspoon chia seeds

Directions:

Place all ingredients in a blender.

Pulse until smooth.

Allow to chill in the fridge before serving.

Nutrition:

Calories 410, Total Fat 20g, Saturated Fat 4g, Total Carbs 47g, Net Carbs 37g, Protein 17g, Sugar: 33g, Fiber: 10g, Sodium: 169mg, Potassium 1163mg

Tropical Carrot Ginger and Turmeric Smoothie

Preparation time: 5 minutes

Cooking time: 0 minutes

Servings: 1

Ingredients:

1 blood orange, peeled and seeded

1 large carrot, peeled and chopped

½ cup frozen mango chunks

2/3 cup coconut water

1 tablespoon raw hemp seeds

¾ teaspoon grated ginger

1 ½ teaspoon peeled and grated turmeric

A pinch of cayenne pepper

A pinch of salt

Directions:

Place all ingredients in a blender and blend until smooth.

Chill before serving.

Nutrition:

Calories 259, Total Fat 6g, Saturated Fat 0.9g, Total Carbs 51g, Net Carbs 40g, Protein 7g, Sugar: 34g, Fiber: 11g, Sodium: 225mg, Potassium 1319mg

Golden Milk Chia Pudding

Preparation time: 6 hours

Cooking time: 0 minutes

Servings: 4

Ingredients:

4 cups coconut milk

3 tablespoons honey

1 teaspoon vanilla extract

1 teaspoon ground turmeric

½ teaspoon ground cinnamon

½ teaspoon ground ginger

¾ cup coconut yogurt

½ cup chia seeds

1 cup fresh mixed berry

¼ cup toasted coconut chips

Directions:

In a mixing bowl, combine the coconut milk, honey, vanilla extract, turmeric, cinnamon, and ginger. Add in the coconut yogurt.

In bowls, place chia seeds, berries, and coconut chips.

Pour in the milk mixture.

Allow to chill in the fridge to set for 6 hours.

Nutrition:

Calories 337, Total Fat 11g, Saturated Fat 2g, Total Carbs 51g, Net Carbs 49g, Protein 10g, Sugar: 29g, Fiber: 2g, Sodium: 262mg, Potassium 508mg

No-Bake Turmeric Protein Donuts

Preparation time: 50 minutes

Cooking time: 0 minutes

Servings: 8

Ingredients:

1 ½ cups raw cashews

½ cup medjool dates, pitted

1 tablespoon vanilla protein powder

½ cup shredded coconut

2 tablespoons maple syrup

¼ teaspoon vanilla extract

1 teaspoon turmeric powder

¼ cup dark chocolate

Directions:

Combine all ingredients except for the chocolate in a food processor.

Pulse until smooth.

Roll batter into 8 balls and press into a silicone donut mold.

Place in the freezer for 30 minutes to set.

Meanwhile, make the chocolate topping by melting the chocolate in a double boiler.

Once the donuts have set, remove the donuts from the mold and drizzle with chocolate.

Nutrition:

Calories 320, Total Fat 26g, Saturated Fat 5g, Total Carbs 20g, Net Carbs 18g, Protein 7g, Sugar: 9g, Fiber: 2g, Sodium:163 mg, Potassium 297mg

Choco-Nana Pancakes

Preparation time: 5 minutes

Cooking time: 6 minutes

Servings: 2

Ingredients:

2 large bananas, peeled and mashed

2 large eggs, pasture-raised

3 tablespoon cacao powder

2 tablespoons almond butter

1 teaspoon pure vanilla extract

1/8 teaspoon salt

Coconut oil for greasing

Directions:

Preheat a skillet on medium low heat and grease the pan with coconut oil.

Place all ingredients in a food processor and pulse until smooth.

Pour a batter (about ¼ cup) onto the skillet and form a pancake.

Cook for 3 minutes on each side.

Nutrition:

Calories 303, Total Fat 17g, Saturated Fat 4g, Total Carbs 36g, Net Carbs 29g, Protein 5g, Sugar: 15g, Fiber: 5g, Sodium: 108mg, Potassium 549mg

Sweet Potato Cranberry Breakfast bars

Preparation time: 10 minutes

Cooking time: 40 minutes

Servings: 8

Ingredients:

1 ½ cups sweet potato puree

2 tablespoons coconut oil, melted

2 tablespoons maple syrup

2 eggs, pasture-raised

1 cup almond meal

1/3 cup coconut flour

1 ½ teaspoon baking soda

1 cup fresh cranberry, pitted and chopped

¼ cup water

Directions:

Preheat the oven to 350oF.

Grease a 9-inch baking pan with coconut oil. Set aside.

In a mixing bowl. Combine the sweet potato puree, water, coconut oil, maple syrup, and eggs.

In another bowl, sift the almond flour, coconut flour, and baking soda.

Gradually add the dry ingredients to the wet ingredients. Use a spatula to fold and mix all ingredients.

Pour into the prepared baking pan and press the cranberries on top.

Place in the oven and bake for 40 minutes or until a toothpick inserted in the middle comes out clean.

Allow to rest or cool before removing from the pan.

Nutrition:

Calories 98, Total Fat 6g, Saturated Fat 1g, Total Carbs 9g, Net Carbs 8.5g, Protein 3g, Sugar: 7g, Fiber: 0.5g, Sodium:113 mg, Potassium 274mg

Savory Breakfast Pancakes

Preparation time: 5 minutes

Cooking time: 6 minutes

Servings: 4

Ingredients:

½ cup almond flour

½ cup tapioca flour

1 cup coconut milk

½ teaspoon chili powder

¼ teaspoon turmeric powder

½ red onion, chopped

1 handful cilantro leaves, chopped

½ inch ginger, grated

1 teaspoon salt

¼ teaspoon ground black pepper

Directions:

In a mixing bowl, mix all ingredients until well-combined.

Heat a pan on low medium heat and grease with oil.

Pour ¼ cup of batter onto the pan and spread the mixture to create a pancake.

Fry for 3 minutes per side.

Repeat until the batter is done.

Nutrition:

Calories 108, Total Fat 2g, Saturated Fat 1g, Total Carbs 20g, Net Carbs 19.5g, Protein 2g, Sugar: 4g, Fiber: 0.5g, Sodium: 37mg, Potassium 95mg

Scrambled Eggs with Smoked Salmon

Preparation time: 10 minutes

Cooking time: 10 minutes

Servings: 2

Ingredients:

4 eggs

2 tablespoons coconut ilk

Fresh chives, chopped

4 slices of wild-caught smoked salmon, chopped

salt to taste

Directions:

In a bowl, whisk the egg, coconut milk, and chives.

Grease the skillet with oil and heat over medium low heat.

Pour the egg mixture and scramble the eggs while cooking.

When the eggs start to settle, add in the smoked salmon and cook for 2 more minutes.

Nutrition:

Calories 349, Total Fat 23g, Saturated Fat 4g, Total Carbs 3g, Net Carbs 1g, Protein 29g, Sugar: 2g, Fiber: 2g, Sodium: 466mg, Potassium 536mg

Raspberry Grapefruit Smoothie

Preparation time: 5 minutes

Cooking time: 0 minutes

Servings: 1

Ingredients:

Juice from 1 grapefruit, freshly squeezed

1 banana, peeled and sliced

1 cup raspberries

Directions:

Place all ingredients in a blender and pulse until smooth.

Chill before serving.

Nutrition:

Calories 381, Total Fat 0.8g, Saturated Fat 0.1g, Total Carbs 96g, Net Carbs 85g, Protein 4g, Sugar: 61g, Fiber: 11g, Sodium: 11mg, Potassium 848mg

Breakfast Burgers with Avocado Buns

Preparation time: 10 minutes

Cooking time: 5 minutes

Servings: 1

Ingredients:

1 ripe avocado

1 egg, pasture-raised

1 red onion slice

1 tomato slice

1 lettuce leaf

Sesame seed for garnish

salt to taste

Directions:

Peel the avocado and remove the seed. Slice the avocado into half. This will serve as the bun. Set aside.

Grease a skillet over medium flame and fry the egg sunny side up for 5 minutes or until set.

Assemble the breakfast burger by placing on top of one avocado half with the egg, red onion, tomato, and lettuce leaf. Top with the remaining avocado bun.

Garnish with sesame seeds on top and season with salt to taste.

Nutrition:

Calories 458, Total Fat 39g, Saturated Fat 4g, Total Carbs 20g, Net Carbs 6g, Protein 13g, Sugar: 8g, Fiber: 14g, Sodium: 118mg, Potassium 1184mg

Spinach Breakfast

Preparation time: 10 minutes

Cooking time: 35minutes

Servings: 4

Ingredients:

2 sweet potatoes, peeled and diced

2 tablespoons olive oil

½ teaspoon onion powder

½ teaspoon garlic powder

¼ teaspoon paprika

4 eggs, pasture-raised

½ onion, sliced

½ cup mushrooms, sliced

2 cups fresh baby spinach

salt and pepper to taste

Coconut oil for greasing

Directions:

Preheat the oven to 4250F.

Place the potatoes in a baking dish and drizzle with olive oil. Season with onion powder, garlic powder, paprika, salt, and pepper to taste. Once cooked, set aside.

Bake in the oven for 30 minutes while turning the sweet potatoes halfway through the cooking time.

Heat skillet and grease with coconut oil.

Sauté the onion for 30 seconds until fragrant.

Add in the mushrooms and egg. Season with salt and pepper to taste.

Scramble the eggs.

Before the eggs have set, stir in the baby spinach until wilted.

Plate the potatoes and top with the egg mixture.

Nutrition:

Calories 252, Total Fat 17g, Saturated Fat 4g, Total Carbs 15g, Net Carbs 13g, Protein 11g, Sugar: 4g, Fiber: 2g, Sodium: 151mg, Potassium 472mg

Avocado Egg

Preparation time: 5 minutes

Cooking time: 20 minutes

Servings: 4

Ingredients:

2 ripe avocados

4 eggs

salt and pepper to taste

Directions:

Preheat the oven to 350oF.

Slice the avocado into half and remove the seed.

Crack one egg into the hollow depression of the avocado where the seed has been.

Season with salt and pepper to taste.

Bake in the oven for 20 minutes or until the eggs have set.

Nutrition:

Calories 290, Total Fat 24g, Saturated Fat 3g, Total Carbs 10g, Net Carbs 3g, Protein 11g, Sugar: 1g, Fiber: 7g, Sodium: 109mg, Potassium 428mg

Healthy Breakfast Chocolate Donuts

Preparation time: 10 minutes

Cooking time: 15 minutes

Servings: 12

Ingredients:

1 cup coconut flour

¼ cup raw cacao powder

½ teaspoon baking soda

4 eggs, pasture-raised

¼ cup coconut oil, melted

¼ cup unsweetened applesauce

1 teaspoon vanilla

¼ cup honey

¼ teaspoon salt

Directions:

Preheat the oven to 350OF.

In a mixing bowl, mix the coconut flour, cacao, baking soda, and salt. Set aside.

In another bowl, mix the eggs, coconut oil, and applesauce. Stir in the vanilla and honey.

Fold the dry ingredients gradually into the wet ingredients until well-combined.

Grease the donut pan with coconut oil.

Press down the dough into the pan.

Bake for 15 minutes or until the dough is cooked through.

Remove from the oven and allow to cool before removing from the donut pan.

Nutrition:

Calories 115, Total Fat 8g, Saturated Fat 4g, Total Carbs 9g, Net Carbs 8.2g, Protein 4g, Sugar: 7g, Fiber: 0.8g, Sodium:108 mg, Potassium 255mg

Baked Eggs with Portobello Mushrooms

Preparation time: 10 minutes

Cooking time: 20 minutes

Servings: 4

Ingredients:

4 portobello mushroom caps

1 cup arugula

1 medium tomato, chopped

4 large eggs, pasture-raised

salt and pepper to taste

Directions:

Preheat the oven to 350oF and line a baking sheet with parchment paper.

Scoop out the gills from the mushrooms using a spoon. Discard the gills and set aside.

Place the mushrooms on the baking sheet inverted (gill side up) and fill each cap with arugula and tomato.

Carefully crack an egg on each mushroom cap.

Bake in the oven for 20 minutes or until the eggs have set.

Nutrition:

Calories 80, Total Fat 5g, Saturated Fat 2g, Total Carbs 5g, Net Carbs 3g, Protein 5g, Sugar: 3g, Fiber: 2g, Sodium: 19mg, Potassium 416mg

Breakfast Spinach Mushroom Tomato Fry Up

Preparation time: 5 minutes

Cooking time: 10 minutes

Servings: 2

Ingredients:

1 teaspoon olive oil

1 red onion, sliced

6 button mushrooms, sliced

½ cup cherry tomatoes, halved

½ teaspoon diced lemon rind

3 large handful baby spinach

salt and pepper to taste

Directions:

Heat oil in a skillet over medium low heat.

Sauté the onion until fragrant.

Add in the mushrooms and tomatoes. Season with lemon rind, salt and pepper. Cook for another 5 minutes.

Stir in the baby spinach until wilted.

Nutrition:

Calories 38, Total Fat 3g, Saturated Fat 0g, Total Carbs 3g, Net Carbs 1.5g, Protein 2g, Sugar: 1g, Fiber: 1.5g, Sodium: 37mg, Potassium 321mg

Sweet Cherry Almond Chia Pudding

Preparation time: 3 hours

Cooking time: 0 minutes

Servings: 4

Ingredients:

2 cups whole sweet cherries, pitted

2 cups coconut milk

¼ cup maple syrup, organic

1 teaspoon vanilla extract

¾ cup chia seeds

½ cup hemp seeds

1/8 teaspoon salt

Directions:

In the blender, combine the cherries, coconut milk, maple syrup, and vanilla extract. Season with salt. Pulse until smooth.

Distribute the chia seeds and hemp seeds in four glasses and pour in the cherry and milk mixture.

Allow to chill in the fridge for 3 hours before serving.

Nutrition:

Calories 302, Total Fat 17g, Saturated Fat 4g, Total Carbs 29g, Net Carbs 22g, Protein 10g, Sugar: 20g, Fiber: 7g, Sodium: 59mg, Potassium 384mg

Pineapple Ginger Smoothie

Preparation time: 5 minutes

Cooking time: 0 minutes

Servings: 1

Ingredients:

1 cup pineapple slice

½ inch thick ginger, sliced

1 cup coconut milk

Directions:

Place all ingredients in a blender.

Pulse until smooth.

Chill before serving.

Nutrition:

Calories 299, Total Fat 8g, Saturated Fat 5g, Total Carbs 51g, Net Carbs 49g, Protein 9g, Sugar: 48g, Fiber: 2g, Sodium: 108mg, Potassium 630mg

Beet and Cherry Smoothie

Preparation time: 5 minutes

Cooking time: 0 minutes

Servings: 4

Ingredients:

10-ounce almond milk, unsweetened

2 small beets, peeled and cut into quarters

½ cup frozen cherries, pitted

½ teaspoon frozen banana

1 tablespoon almond butter

Directions:

Add all ingredients in a blender.

Blend until smooth.

Nutrition:

Calories 470, Total Fat 38g, Saturated Fat 6g, Total Carbs 24g, Net Carbs 14g, Protein 16g, Sugar: 10g, Fiber: 10g, Sodium: 67mg, Potassium 733mg

Spicy Pineapple Smoothie

Preparation time: 5 minutes

Cooking time: 0 minutes

Servings: 1

Ingredients:

1 tablespoon chia seeds

1 teaspoon black pepper powder

1 orange, peeled

1 ½ cups frozen pineapple chunks

1 cup coconut water

1 teaspoon ground turmeric

Directions:

Place all ingredients in a blender.

Pulse until smooth.

Serve chilled.

Nutrition:

Calories 378, Total Fat 10g, Saturated Fat 2g, Total Carbs 73g, Net Carbs 53g, Protein 9g, Sugar: 42g, Fiber: 20g, Sodium: 261mg, Potassium 1281mg

Breakfast Cherry Muffins

Preparation time: 10 minutes

Cooking time: 30 minutes

Servings: 6

Ingredients:

1 ½ cup almond flour

¼ cup arrowroot flour

¼ cup coconut oil

¼ cup maple syrup

3 whole eggs

2 teaspoons vanilla extract

1 ½ teaspoons almond extract

1 teaspoon baking powder

1 cup fresh cherry, pitted and chopped

¼ teaspoon salt

Directions:

Preheat the oven to 350oF.

In a mixing bowl, combine all ingredients except for the cherries. Mix until well-combined.

Add the cherries last.

Fill muffin liners with the batter and bake for 30 minutes or until a toothpick inserted comes out clean.

Nutrition:

Calories 528, Total Fat 39g, Saturated Fat 5g, Total Carbs 36g, Net Carbs 29g, Protein 13g, Sugar: 15g, Fiber: 7g, Sodium: 177mg, Potassium 679mg

Breakfast Shakshuka

Preparation time: 5 minutes

Cooking time: 10 minutes

Servings: 6

Ingredients:

1 tablespoon olive oil

½ onion, chopped

1 clove garlic, minced

1 red bell pepper, seeded and chopped

4 cups tomatoes, diced

1 teaspoon chili powder

1 teaspoon paprika

6 eggs, pasture-raised

½ tablespoon fresh parsley, chopped

salt and pepper to taste

Directions:

Heat oil in a skillet over medium flame.

Sauté the onion and garlic for 30 seconds or until fragrant.

Add in the red bell pepper and tomatoes. Season with salt and pepper to taste. Stir in the chili powder and paprika. Allow to simmer until the tomatoes are soft.

Reduce the heat and create 6 wells in the skillet.

Crack in one egg in each well and increase the heat.

Cover and allow to simmer for 5 minutes.

Garnish with parsley last.

Nutrition:

Calories 177, Total Fat 12g, Saturated Fat 3g, Total Carbs 7g, Net Carbs 5g, Protein 10g, Sugar: 4g, Fiber: 2g, Sodium:109 mg, Potassium 445mg

Anti-Inflammatory Crepes

Preparation time: 5 minutes

Cooking time: 4 minutes

Servings: 4

Ingredients:

2 tablespoon coconut flour

4 large eggs, pasture-raised

1 tablespoon coconut oil

1 cup hazelnuts, soaked in water overnight

2/3 cup dark chocolates

½ teaspoon vanilla extract

2 tablespoon maple syrup

½ cup water

Directions:

Preheat the oven to 350oF.

In a bowl, mix the coconut flour, eggs, and water until well-combined.

Heat oil in a skillet over medium flame and grease the skillet with coconut oil.

Scoop 1/3 cup of the crepe mixture into the skillet and cook for 4 minutes while flipping halfway through the cooking time.

Repeat until all batter is made into crepes.

Make the hazelnut sauce by combining the hazelnuts, dark chocolates, vanilla extract, and maple syrup in a blender.

Pulse until smooth.

Spread the Nutella sauce over the crepes before serving.

Nutrition:

Calories 465, Total Fat 29g, Saturated Fat 6g, Total Carbs 46g, Net Carbs g, Protein 9g, Sugar: 32g, Fiber: 5g, Sodium: 53mg, Potassium 401mg

Blueberry Hemp Seed Smoothie

Preparation time: 5 minutes

Cooking time: 0 minutes

Servings: 1

Ingredients:

1 ¼ cup frozen blueberries

2 tablespoons hemp seeds

1 serving vanilla plant-based protein powder

½ cup packed fresh spinach

1 teaspoon spirulina powder

1 ¼ unsweetened plant-based milk

¼ teaspoon holy basil leaves, chopped

Directions:

Place all ingredients in a blender.

Blend until smooth.

Nutrition:

Calories 442, Total Fat 19g, Saturated Fat 5g, Total Carbs 50g, Net Carbs 43g, Protein 27g, Sugar: 33g, Fiber: 7g, Sodium: 426mg, Potassium 960mg

Chickpea Scramble with Kale

Preparation time: 5 minutes

Cooking time: 5 minutes

Servings: 2

Ingredients:

1 cup chickpea flour

1 teaspoon turmeric powder

1 tablespoon nutritional yeast

1 tablespoon olive oil

½ small onion, diced

4 cloves of garlic, minced

1 bunch kale, torn into small pieces

½ cup water

½ teaspoon salt

Directions:

Mix the chickpea flour and water until well-combined. Season with salt, turmeric powder, and nutritional yeast.

Heat oil in a skillet over medium flame.

Sauté the onion and garlic until fragrant.

Stir in the kale for 30 seconds.

Pour in the chickpea mixture and continue mixing for 3 minutes or until the chickpea eggs have set.

Nutrition:

Calories 279, Total Fat10 g, Saturated Fat 1g, Total Carbs 34g, Net Carbs 27g, Protein 14g, Sugar: 6g, Fiber: 7g, Sodium: 301mg, Potassium 698mg

Quick and Creamy Whole Grain Porridge

Preparation time: 5 minutes

Cooking time: 5 minutes

Servings: 2

Ingredients:

½ cup cooked quinoa

¼ cup sunflower seeds

¼ cup raw walnuts

2 tablespoons chopped dates

1 teaspoon cinnamon

¼ cup almond milk

1 tablespoon raw honey

½ diced apple

1 tablespoon chia seeds

Directions:

In a saucepan, add the quinoa, sunflower seeds, walnuts, dates, cinnamon, milk, and raw honey.

Heat over medium flame. Add more water or water to achieve a porridge consistency.

Before serving, stir in apple and chia seeds last.

Nutrition:

Calories 317, Total Fat 17g, Saturated Fat 2g, Total Carbs 39g, Net Carbs 33g, Protein 8g, Sugar: 22g, Fiber: 6g, Sodium: 27mg, Potassium 365mg

Omega-3 Chocolate Chia Hemp Pudding

Preparation time: 5 minutes

Cooking time: 0 minutes

Servings: 1

Ingredients:

2 tablespoons chia seeds

2 tablespoons hemp seeds

1 tablespoon cacao powder

6 small pitted dates, chopped

½ cup unsweetened almond milk

½ teaspoon pure vanilla extract

1 tablespoon chocolate protein powder

¼ teaspoon salt

Directions:

Add all ingredients in a blender and pulse until smooth.

Pour into individual containers and place inside the fridge for at least 2 hours before serving.

Nutrition:

Calories 367, Total Fat 13g, Saturated Fat 1g, Total Carbs 55 g, Net Carbs 47g, Protein 12g, Sugar: 39g, Fiber: 8g, Sodium: 129mg, Potassium 686mg

No Bake Granola Breakfast Bars

Preparation time: 2 hours 15 minutes

Cooking time: 0 minutes

Servings: 6

Ingredients:

2 cups raisins, soaked in water then drained

3 tablespoons pure maple syrup

½ cup tahini or almond butter

2 cups oats

1 cup raw sunflower seeds

½ cup cacao nibs

Directions:

Mix all ingredients in mixing bowl until well-combined.

Press firmly into a parchment-lined baking pan.

Allow to set in the fridge for two hours.

Remove from the pan once set and slice into bars.

Nutrition:

Calories 372, Total Fat 26g, Saturated Fat 3g, Total Carbs 36g, Net Carbs 27g, Protein 15g, Sugar: 9g, Fiber: 9g, Sodium: 52mg, Potassium 511mg

Anti-Inflammatory Energy Bars

Preparation time: 15 minutes

Cooking time: 0 minutes

Servings: 5

Ingredients:

1 ¼ cup packed dates, pitted and chopped

1 cup unsweetened fine coconut meat

1 cup hemp seeds

2/3 cup cashew nuts, toasted and chopped

2 tablespoons coconut oil

Directions:

Place all ingredients in a food processor until well-combined.

Line a baking dish with parchment paper and press the dough into the pan.

Place in the fridge for an hour to set.

Once frozen, lift the bars out of the pan and cut into 10 squares.

Nutrition:

Calories 471, Total Fat 34g, Saturated Fat 6g, Total Carbs 41g, Net Carbs 34g, Protein 10g, Sugar: 26g, Fiber: 7g, Sodium:60 mg, Potassium 588mg

No-Bake Chocolate Chia Energy Bars

Preparation time: 10 minutes

Cooking time: 0 minutes

Servings: 5

Ingredients:

1 ½ cups pitted dates, chopped

1/3 cup cacao powder

½ cup whole chia seeds

½ cup shredded coconut

1 cup raw walnut, chopped

½ cup dark chocolate bar, chopped

½ cup oats

½ teaspoon vanilla extract

¼ teaspoon salt

Directions:

Place all ingredients in a food processor and pulse until a thick dough is formed.

Line a baking pan with parchment paper.

Press the dough into the pan.

Place inside the fridge to allow to set for at least 2 hours.

Once hardened, slice into 10 bars.

Nutrition:

Calories 284, Total Fat 12g, Saturated Fat 1g, Total Carbs 45g, Net Carbs g, Protein 5g, Sugar: 32g, Fiber: 6g, Sodium: 40mg, Potassium 506mg

Breakfast Oatmeal Raisin Bars

Preparation time: 2 hours 15 minutes

Cooking time: 0 minutes

Servings: 8

Ingredients:

3 cups dates, pitted and chopped

2 cups oats

½ cup chocolate chips, organic

½ cup raisins

½ teaspoon salt

Directions:

Place all ingredients in a food processor and pulse until a thick dough is formed.

Line a baking pan with parchment paper.

Press the dough into the pan.

Place inside the fridge to allow to set for at least 2 hours.

Once hardened, slice into 16 bars.

Nutrition:

Calories 235, Total Fat 3g, Saturated Fat 1g, Total Carbs 59g, Net Carbs 51g, Protein 6g, Sugar: 36g, Fiber: 8g, Sodium: 3mg, Potassium 520 mg

Tropical Chia Seed Oats

Preparation time: 2 hours 15 minutes

Cooking time: 0 minutes

Servings: 1

Ingredients:

½ cup quick oats

1 cup diced fresh pineapples

1 tablespoon chia seeds

1 cup unsweetened almond milk

½ teaspoon pure vanilla extract

1 sliced banana

2 tablespoons toasted coconut

Directions:

In a container, place the oats, pineapples, chia seeds, almond milk, and vanilla. Stir to combine everything.

Place inside the fridge for at least 2 hours.

Once ready, top with banana and toasted coconut.

Nutrition:

Calories 535, Total Fat 14g, Saturated Fat 4g, Total Carbs 89g, Net Carbs76 g, Protein 17g, Sugar: 42g, Fiber: 13g, Sodium: 142mg, Potassium 1129mg

Quinoa Breakfast Bowl

Preparation time: 10 minutes

Cooking time: 15 minutes

Servings: 1

Ingredients:

¼ cup quinoa, rinsed

2 tablespoons dried goji berries

1 small banana, peeled and sliced

¼ cup fresh blueberries

1 tablespoon chopped walnuts

1 tablespoon slivered almonds

1 tablespoon pumpkin seeds, hulled

¼ cup unsweetened almond milk

1 tablespoon maple syrup

1/8 teaspoon ground cinnamon

1/8 teaspoon vanilla extract

¾ cup water

Directions:

Bring water to a boil in a small pot and add quinoa. Cook for 12 to 15 minutes then drain.

Allow the quinoa to cool. Fluff it and place in a bowl.

Top with goji berries, banana, blueberries, walnuts, almond, and pumpkin seed.

Pour over almond milk and maple syrup.

Dust with cinnamon and flavor with vanilla extract.

Nutrition:

Calories 516, Total Fat 13g, Saturated Fat 1g, Total Carbs 94g, Net Carbs 85g, Protein 13g, Sugar: 47g, Fiber: 9g, Sodium: 70mg, Potassium 949mg

Quinoa Bowls Avocado Egg

Preparation time: 10 minutes

Cooking time: 10 minutes

Servings: 1

Ingredients:

2 teaspoons extra virgin olive oil

2 large eggs, pasture-raised

1 cup grape tomatoes, halve

1 teaspoon red wine vinegar

1 cup cooked quinoa

½ cup black beans, cooked

2 tablespoons chopped cilantro

½ ripe avocado, sliced

What you'll need from the store cupboard:

¼ teaspoon salt

Directions:

Heat oil in a skillet over medium flame.

Fry the eggs for 3 minutes. Set aside.

Using the same skillet, sauté the tomatoes for 3 minutes until wilted.

Add in the red wine vinegar and season with salt and pepper to taste. Set aside.

Assemble the bowl by putting the quinoa in a bowl and top with beans and tomatoes. Add in the eggs and avocado.

Garnish with avocado slices.

Nutrition:

Calories 343, Total Fat 16g, Saturated Fat 3.1 g, Total Carbs 35g, Net Carbs 26g, Protein 15g, Sugar: 3g, Fiber: 9g, Sodium: 332mg, Potassium 893mg

Anti-Inflammatory Porridge

Preparation time: 2 hours and 10 minutes

Cooking time: 10 minutes

Servings: 2

Ingredients:

2 tablespoons hemp seeds

¼ cup walnuts, chopped

¼ cup toasted coconuts

¼ cup unsweetened almond milk

¼ cup coconut milk

¼ cup almond butter

1 tablespoon extra-virgin coconut oil

¼ teaspoon ground turmeric

1 teaspoon bee pollen

¼ teaspoon cinnamon

2 tablespoons chia seeds

Directions:

Roast the hemp seeds, walnuts, and coconuts in a skillet until toasted. Set aside.

In the same skillet, heat the almond milk, coconut milk, and almond butter until everything is combined. Set aside and allow to cool.

To the milk mixture, add in the coconut oil, turmeric, bee pollen, and cinnamon.

Assemble the porridge by putting the toasted nuts at the bottom of the bowl.

Add in chia seeds.

: Pour in the milk mixture.

Allow to soak in the fridge for at least 2 hours.

Nutrition:

Calories 575, Total Fat 50g, Saturated Fat 4g, Total Carbs 6g, Net Carbs 4g, Protein 15g, Sugar: 4g, Fiber: 2g, Sodium: 57mg, Potassium 645 mg

Ginger Turmeric Oatmeal

Preparation time: 8 hours and 5 minutes

Cooking time: 0 minutes

Servings: 2

Ingredients:

1 cup rolled oats

2 tablespoons maple syrup

¼ teaspoon ground turmeric

¼ teaspoon ground ginger

1 cup frozen assorted berries

½ cup water

A pinch of black of pepper

Directions:

Mix the oats with water, maple, turmeric, black pepper, and ginger until well-combined.

Add in the berries.

Allow to sit in the fridge overnight.

Nutrition:

Calories 280, Total Fat 6g, Saturated Fat 3g, Total Carbs 64g, Net Carbs 57g, Protein 11g, Sugar: 30g, Fiber: 7g, Sodium: 59mg, Potassium 456mg

Chapter 6. Main Dishes

Quick and Easy Quinoa Orange Salad

Preparation time:40 mins, Serves: Serves 1

Ingredients

1 cup cooked quinoa, cooled

2 small oranges, supremed

1 celery rib, finely chopped

20g Brazil nuts, chopped

1 green onion, sliced

¼ cup fresh parsley, finely chopped

For the dressing

juice from above oranges

½ tsp lemon juice

½ tsp fresh ginger, grated

1 tsp white wine vinegar

1 small clove garlic, minced

½ tsp salt

¼ tsp black pepper

pinch cinnamon

Directions:

Cut the oranges into supreme bits, work over a pan, so that no juice is lost. Ensure to squeeze all the juice out of the "membranes" left behind when you've done all of your supremes.

Move the juice to your food processor or mini blender. Add the remaining dressing ingredients and combine until smooth.

Cut your supreme orange into bits of bite size and add them to a mixing bowl of medium size. Add remaining ingredients & stir until well mixed, including the dressing.

Serve immediately or hold until ready to serve in the refrigerator.

Nutrition:

Calories: 208, Fat: 8g, Sodium: 34mg, Carbohydrates: 40g, Fiber: 4.3g, Sugar: 4.2g, Protein: 6.7g

Herb-Crusted Cauliflower Steaks with Beans and Tomatoes

Prep/Cook Time 45 minutes

Servings:

Ingredients

8 ounces green beans, trimmed

3 garlic cloves, finely chopped

2 teaspoons kosher salt, divided

1 teaspoon freshly ground black pepper, divided

1/3 cp chopped parsley, plus more for serving

1/3 cp panko (Japanese breadcrumbs)

1/4 cp freshly grated Parmesan

1 (15-oz) can white beans, rinsed, drained

1 cp golden or red cherry tomatoes (about 6 ounces), halved

3/4 tsp. finely grated lemon zest

1 large head of cauliflower (around 2 pounds)

1/2 cp olive oil, divided

3 tablespoons mayonnaise

1 tsp. Dijon mustard

Directions:

In the middle and upper third of the oven, place racks; preheat to 425 ° F. Remove the leaves and trim the coliflower end of the stem, leaving the core intact. Place the core of the cauliflower down on a surface of work. Using a large knife, cut to produce 2 (1)" "steaks "in the middle from top to bottom; reserve the remaining cauliflower for further use.

Place the coliflower on a baking sheet with an edge. Brush with 1 Tbsp on both ends. Oil; 1/4 tsp. season. Salt, 1/4 tsp. Pepper, pepper. Roast on the middle rack, rotating for about 30 minutes, until the cauliflower is tender and black.

While, add 1 Tbsp of green beans. Gas, 1/2 c.p. Oil, 1/4 tablespoon. Pepper on a rimmed sheet of baking. Set aside in one layer, then roast in the upper third of the oven until green beans start blistering, about 15 minutes.

Whisk garlic, lemon zest, petroleum 1/3 cup, and 6 Tbsp remaining. 1 1/4 tsp of fuel. Oil, 1/2 tablespoon. Pepper until smooth in a medium bowl. Put half of the mixture to a medium bowl. In the first tub, add panko and parmesan and combine with your hands. In the second bowl, add the white beans and tomatoes and toss to coat. In a small bowl, whisk the mayonnaise and mustard.

Remove from the oven the sheets. Spread the mixture of mayonnaise over the coliflower. Sprinkle evenly over the cauliflower 1/4 cup panko mixture. Add white bean mixture with green beans to the sheet and blend together. Return the sheets to the oven and continue to roast until the white beans start to crisp and the panko topping begins to brown for another 5–7 minutes.

Divide between plates cauliflower, green beans, white beans and tomatoes. Top with petersil.

Note In order to cut big, 1 "steaks from a cauliflower head, the center root must remain intact. Use 2 large cauliflower heads to serve 4.

Nutrition:

Calories 1141, Carbohydrates 89 g, Fat 77 g, Protein 34 g, Saturated Fat 13 g, Sodium 2287 mg, Fiber 25 g, Cholestero l18 mg.

5 Ingredient Thai Pumpkin Soup

Preparation time: 15 minutes

Servings: 2

Ingredients

1 3/4 cup coconut milk/a 13.5 oz can, reserving 1 tablespoon

1 large red chili pepper sliced

2 tbspoons red curry paste

4 cups chicken/vegetable broth about 32 oz

2 15 oz cans pumpkin puree

cilantro for garnish if desired

Directions:

Cook the curry paste for about a minute or until the paste is fragrant in a large saucepan over medium heat. Add the pumpkin and the broth and mix.

Cook for about 3 minutes or until bubble starts in the broth. Add the milk of the coconut and cook for about 3 minutes until warm.

Garnish with a drizzle of coconut milk reserved and sliced red chilis in cups. Garnish with leaves of coriander if desired.

Nutrition:

Calories 141, Carbohydrates 19 g, Fat 55 g, Protein 30 g

Mediterranean Tuna Salad

Preparation time:10 minutes

Servings: 2

Ingredients

2 Tablespoons chopped fire roasted red peppers

2 Tablespoons chopped fresh basil

1 Tablespoon capers

2, 5ounces cans tuna packed in water, drained

1/4 cp mayonnaise

1/4 cp chopped kalamata or mixed olives

2 Tablespoons minced red onion

1 Tablespoon fresh lemon juice

salt and pepper

2 large vine-ripened tomatoes

Directions:

In the large bowl, add all the ingredients except the tomatoes and stir to combine. Slice the tomatoes into sixths, without slicing through all the way, and then open gently. Then serve the mixture of Scoop Mediterranean Tuna Salad in the middle.

Notes: Could also serve tuna salad as a sandwich, in a pita pocket, on a bed of greens, or with crackers.

Nutrition:

Calories 115, Carbohydrates 14 g, Fat 7.7 g, Protein g, Saturated Fat 13 g, Sodium 2287 mg, Fiber 25 g, Cholesterol l18 mg.

Red Lentil and Squash Curry Stew

Preparation time: 40 minutes

Servings: 2

Ingredients:

1 tabsp good quality curry powder (or more to taste)

1 carton broth (4 cups) I used low-sodium

1 cup red lentils

1 tsp Extra virgin olive oil

1 sweet onion, chopped

1 cup greens of choice

Fresh grated ginger, to taste (this is optional)

Kosher salt & black pepper, to taste

3 garlic cloves, minced

3 cups cooked butternut squash

Directions:

Add EVOO and chopped onion and chopped garlic in a large pot. Saute over low-medium heat for about 5 minutes.

Remove the curry powder and cook for a few more minutes. Remove lentils and broth and bring to a boil. Reduce heat for 10 minutes and cook.

Add cooked butternut squash and choice vegetables. Cook around 5-8 minutes over medium heat. Season with salt, pepper and apply to taste some freshly grated ginger.

Nutrition:

Calories: 302, Fat: 12g, Carbohydrates: 22g, Fiber: 5g, Sugar: 2g, Protein: 22g

Lemon-Herb Sardine Salad

Preparation time:10 minutes

Servings: 2

Ingredients

Two 4.4-oz cans olive-oil-packed (drained) sardines

Coarse salt and freshly ground black pepper

Great Value Salt, 26 oz

1 tablespoon rinsed capers

2 tablespoons chopped fresh parsley

1 tablespoon chopped fresh tarragon

2 finely diced stalks celery

2 tablespoons extra-virgin olive oil

1 teaspoon grated lemon zest

Juice of 1 lemon

1 teaspoon Dijon mustard

Lettuce, for serving

Directions:

In a pan, mix butter, lemon zest, water, mustard, capers, parsley, tarragon, and celery.

Fold gently in sardines and use salt and pepper to season. Serve with lettuce.

Nutrition:

Calories: 160, Fat: 22g, Sodium: 35mg, Carbohydrates: 12g, Fiber: 13g, Sugar: 2g, Protein: 16g

Buddha Bowl with Orange, Kale, Avocado and Wild Rice

Preparation time: 40 minutes

Servings:

Ingredients

2 tablespoons extra-virgin olive oil

2 tablespoons rice vinegar

1 tablespoon chopped fresh mint

Rice

1 cup wild rice

3 cups vegetable broth or water

1 garlic clove, minced

Salt and freshly ground black pepper

Toppings

1 orange, cut into segments

½ avocado, sliced

¼ cup pumpkin seeds

1 bunch kale, roughly chopped

2 tablespoons olive oil

1 tablespoon rice vinegar

¼ cup pomegranate seeds

2 hard-boiled eggs

Salt and freshly ground black pepper

Directions:

Make the rice: combine the rice with the broth (or liquid, if used) and garlic in a medium dish. Take the mixture over medium - high heat to a simmer

Once the water is boiling, reduce the heat to low and simmer for 15 to 17 minutes until the rice is tender & all the liquid is absorbed.

Cook the rice for 5 to 10 minutes, then add the olive oil, vinegar, basil, salt and pepper.

Create the Toppings: shake the kale with the olive oil and vinegar in a medium bowl. Divide the rice into two bowls and finish with the same volume of kale.

Top of the bowl with 2 tablespoons of pomegranate seeds, half of the orange slices, half of the slices of avocado, 2 tablespoons of pumpkin seeds, and a hard-boiled egg. Add salt and pepper to the egg. Serve right away.

Nutrition:

417 calories, 15g fat, 12g protein, 62g carbs, 2g sugars

Kale, Chickpea and Tomato Stew Recipe

Preparation time: 40 minutes

Servings: 4

Ingredients

4 Tbsp. olive oil, divided

1 medium onion, cut into eighths

1 1/4 tsp. kosher salt, divided

6 garlic cloves, thinly sliced

1/4 tsp. crushed red pepper flakes

3/4 pound kale, stems removed & leaves coarsely chopped

1 pound tomatoes (about 3 medium), cored and chopped

2 (15-ounce) cans chickpeas, drained and rinsed

1 cup vegetable stock

4 large eggs

Directions:

Heat 2 Tbsp in a big pan. Oil at medium at low heat. Add 1/4 tsp of onion. Salt and cook for about 7 minutes until tender. Remove flakes of garlic and red pepper and cook for another 2 minutes. Remove kale and stir for about 2 minutes until wilted. Add tomatoes, chickpeas and stock; cook over medium heat until the tomatoes break down for about 10 minutes. 3/4 tsp salt to season.

Heat remaining 2 Tbsp in a large nonstick skillet. Medium heat oil. Crack 2 eggs and cook for about 3 minutes until slightly crisp on the bottom and white. Take to a plate and repeat with 2 eggs left over. Stew spoon into 4 shallow bowls, each with a fried egg on top, sprinkle with 1/4 tsp remaining salt and serve.

Nutrition: Calories: 188, Fat: 3.8g, Sodium: 145mg, Carbohydrates: 3g, Fiber: 3.3g, Sugar: 12g, Protein: 25g

Smoked Salmon Potato Tartine

Preparation time: 45 minutes

Servings:

Ingredients

Potato Tartine:

1 large russet potato, peeled & grated lengthwise

2 tbspoons clarified butter (or other neutral flavored oil)

salt

pepper

Toppings:

1/2 garlic clove, finely minced

zest of half a lemon

1/2 hard boiled egg, finely chopped

thinly sliced smoked salmon

2 tablespoons drained capers

2 tablespoons finely chopped red onion

4ounces soft goat cheese, at room temperature

1 1/2 tbspoons finely minced chives

finely minced chives (for garnish)

Directions:

Assemble Toppings:

In a small bowl, mix goat's cheese, lemon zest and garlic. Season to taste with salt and pepper. Stir gently in the fresh chives. Put it aside.

Season the chopped onion with salt and the hard-boiled egg.

Prepare Potato Tartine:

Work quickly (as the potato starts to oxidize quickly), grate the potato (lengthwise) into a large one using a grater's large holes. To remove any excess water, squeeze the potatoes over the sink. Season with salt and pepper and toss generously.

Heat clarified butter over medium - high heat in an 8-10-inch non-stick skillet. When it hot, add the grated potato and shape roughly to a large circle using a spatula.

To compact, cover and cook gently for 8-10 minutes or until the bottom is golden brown, press the mixture with back of a spoon.

Flip to the other side carefully and cook for another 8-10 minutes or until golden brown and crispy.

Remove from the rack to cool and allow to cool until the temperature is barely lukewarm or room.

Assemble Tartine: spread the goat cheese mixture over the top once the potato cake has cooled. Spoon directly over the smoked salmon and scatter with the red onion, hard-boiled egg, and capers. Garnish with chives that have been freshly cut.

Cut into wedges and serve as soon as possible.

Nutrition:

Calories: 304, Fat: 8g, Sodium: 115mg, Carbohydrates: 6g, Fiber: 2g, Sugar: 1.2g, Protein: 4.7g

Kale Caesar Salad with Grilled Chicken Wrap

Preparation time:15 minutes

Servings: 2

Ingredients

1 cup cherry tomatoes, quartered

3/4 cup finely shredded Parmesan cheese

½ coddled egg (cooked about 1 minute)

1 clove garlic, minced

8 oz grilled chicken, thinly sliced

6 cups curly kale, cut into bite sized pieces

1/2 teaspoon Dijon mustard

1 teaspoon honey or agave

1/8 cup fresh lemon juice

1/8 cup olive oil

Kosher salt and freshly ground black pepper

2 Lavash flat breads or two large tortillas

Directions:

Mix half of a coddled potato, chopped garlic, mustard, butter, lemon juice and olive oil together in a pan. Whisk until a dressing has been created. Season with salt and pepper to taste.

Add the tomatoes of broccoli, chicken and cherry and toss to coat with the shredded parmesan dressing and ¼ cup.

Layer the two flatbreads of the lavash. Spread the salad evenly over the two wraps and sprinkle with ¼ cup of parmesan each.

Roll up and slice half of the wraps. Eat right away

Nutrition:

Calories: 190, Fat: 6g, Sodium: 120mg, Carbohydrates: 6g, Fiber: 3g, Sugar: 1.4g, Protein: 30g

Roasted Red Pepper and Sweet Potato Soup

Preparation time: 55 minutes

Servings: 6

Ingredients

1 can (4 oz) diced green chiles

2 tsp.s ground cumin

1 tsp. salt

1 tsp. ground coriander

3 to 4 cups peeled, cubed sweet potatoes

2 tbsp. olive oil

2 medium onions, chopped

1 jar (12ounces) roasted red peppers, chopped, liquid reserved

4 cups vegetable broth

2 tbsps. minced fresh cilantro

1 tbsp. lemon juice

4 oz cream cheese, cubed

Directions:

Heat the olive oil over medium - high heat in a large soup pot or Dutch oven. Incorporate the onion and cook until soft. Add chilies, cumin, salt and coriander in the red peppers. Cook for about 1-2 minutes.

In the roasted red peppers, vegetable broth, and sweet potatoes add the reserved juice. Take to a boil, then lower heat and cover. Cook for 10-15 minutes until the potatoes are tender. Stir in the juice of the coriander and the lemon. Let the soup cool down a little bit.

Layer half of the soup with the cream cheese in a blender. Process until smooth, then add back and heat through the soup pot. Season with extra salt if necessary.

Nutrition:

Calories: 278, Fat: 9g, Protein: 11g

Lettuce Wraps with Smoked Trout

Preparation time: 45 minutes

Servings: 2

Ingredients

1/2 unpeeled English hothouse cucumber (don't remove seeds)

1/4 cp thinly sliced shallots

1/4 cp thinly sliced jalapeño chiles with seeds (preferably red; about 2 large)

2 4.5-oz packages skinless smoked trout fillets, broken into bite-size pieces (upto 2 cups)

2 tblpoons fresh lime juice or unseasoned rice vinegar

1 tbspoon sugar

1 tbspoon fish sauce (such as nam pla or nuoc nam)

2 medium carrots, peeled

1 cp diced grape tomatoes

1/3 cp Asian sweet chili sauce

1/4 cp finely chopped lightly salted dry-roasted peanuts

1/2 cup whole fresh mint leaves

1/2 cup small whole fresh basil leaves

16 small to medium inner leaves of romaine lettuce (from about 2 hearts of romaine)

Directions:

Rasp carrots and cucumber lengthwise into ribbons using vegetable peeler. Cut ribbons into sections of 3 inches, then cut sections into strips of match-stick length. Set in a big bowl. Add jalapeños, sugar, shallots, lime juice, and fish sauce and marinate at room temperature for 30 minutes.

Add bits of trout and tomatoes to the mixture of vegetables and blend together. Transfer the mixture of trout and vegetables to the large strainer and drain the liquid. Return the mixture of trout and vegetable to the same bowl; add mint and basil and mix.

Arrange the leaves of lettuce on the large plate. Divide the lettuce leaves in the salad of the broccoli. Sprinkle each salad with sweet chili sauce and sprinkle with peanuts.

Nutrition:

Calories 423, Carbohydrates 60 g, Fat 12 g, Protein 33 g, Saturated Fat 2 g, Sodium 1245 mg

Lentil, Beetroot and Hazelnut Salad and a Ginger Dressing

Preparation time: 10 minutes

Servings: 2–3

Ingredients

  For the salad:

2 spring onions, finely sliced

2 tablepoons hazelnuts, roughly chopped

A handful of fresh mint, roughly chopped

A handful of fresh parsley, roughly chopped

1 cup Puy lentils, rinsed

2 3/4 cup filtered water

Sea salt

3 cooked beetroot, cut into small cubes

  For the ginger dressing:

1 teaspoon Dijon mustard

1 tablespoon apple cider vinegar

3/4 inch cube of fresh ginger, peeled and roughly chopped

6 tbpoons olive oil

Pinch of sea salt then freshly ground black pepper

Directions:

Place them in a saucepan for the lentils, cover with water, bring the heat to the boil then simmer for about 15 minutes–20 minutes, or until all liquid has evaporated and lentils are not mushy & still with a bite.

Transfer them to a big bowl as soon as the lentils are cooked and leave to cool.

Adding the beetroot, hazelnuts, spring onions, and herbs once the lentils are cool and stir until all is mixed.

Put the ginger, oil, mustard and vinegar in a bowl for the dressing and mix until combined with a handheld blender.

Drizzle and serve the dressing over the salad.

Nutrition:

Calories 815, Carbohydrates 78 g, Fat 46 g, Protein 28 g, Saturated Fat 6 g, Sodium 1486 mg

Chapter 7. Snacks & Appetizers

Spiced Kale Chips

Preparation Time: 10 Minutes

Cooking Time: 20 Minutes

Servings: 4

Ingredients:

1 Bunch of Kale, washed & patted dry

1/8 tsp. Garlic Powder

¼ tsp. Salt

1/8 tsp. Black Pepper

¼ tsp. Cayenne Pepper, grounded

1 tsp. Oil

Directions:

Preheat the oven to 300 ° F.

After that, tear off the kale leaves and place them on a wire rack, which is on top of a foil-lined baking sheet.

Now, apply oil in your hands and massage them on the leaves. Tip: You need to use the oil only lightly.

Top it with salt, pepper, and cayenne pepper.

Finally, bake them for 20 minutes or until the edges are crispy.

Tip: If you wish it to be spicier, you can add more cayenne pepper.

Nutrition:

Calories: 25Kcal

Proteins:1g

Carbohydrates: 3g

Fat: 1g

Vegetable Nuggets

Preparation Time: 10 Minutes

Cooking Time: 25 Minutes

Servings: Makes 24

Ingredients:

¼ tsp. Black Pepper

2 cups Cauliflower Florets

1 Egg, large & pastured

2 cups Broccoli Florets

½ cup Almond Meal

1 cup Carrots, chopped coarsely

¼ tsp. Salt

1 tsp. Garlic, minced

½ tsp. Turmeric, grounded

Directions:

To make these tasty nuggets, you first need to preheat the oven to 400 ° F.

Next, place broccoli, turmeric, cauliflower, black pepper, carrots, sea salt, and turmeric in a food processor.

Pulse them for a minute or until you get a finely grounded mixture.

Then, stir in the almond meal and egg into it and pulse them again until mixed.

Now, transfer the veggie-almond mixture to a large mixing bowl.

Scoop out the mixture with a tablespoon and make circular discs with your hands.

After that, place the discs on the parchment paper-lined baking sheet.

Finally, bake them for 20 to 25 minutes while flipping it once.

Tip: Serve it along with homemade ranch sauce.

Nutrition:

Calories: 22Kcal

Proteins:1.1g

Carbohydrates: 2.1g

Fat: 1.2g

Cabbage Pineapple Slaw

Preparation Time: 10 Minutes

Cooking Time: 35 Minutes

Servings: 12 to 14

Ingredients:

2 Red Bell Peppers, sliced thinly

½ of 1 Purple Cabbage, thinly sliced

1 cup Cilantro, sliced thinly

½ of 1 Red Cabbage, sliced thinly

3 cups Pineapple, chopped

For the sauce:

1 cup Cashews, soaked

½ tsp. Red Pepper Flakes

½ cup Water

2-inches Ginger

1 tbsp. + 1 tsp. Lime Juice

Salt & Pepper, to taste

Directions:

To begin with, place all the ingredients needed to make the sauce in a high-speed blender until you get a smooth sauce.

After that, place both the cabbage slices, pineapple, and red peppers in a large mixing bowl. Toss well.

To this, spoon in the cashew sauce and toss them again.

Serve immediately or keep in refrigerator until served.

Tip: You can even add tuna or chicken to this salad for a main dish.

Nutrition:

Calories: 22Kcal

Proteins:1.1g

Carbohydrates: 2.1g

Fat: 1.2g

Turmeric Muffins

Preparation Time: 10 Minutes

Cooking Time: 25 Minutes

Servings: Makes 8 Muffins

Ingredients:

¾ cup + 2 tbsp. Coconut Flour

6 Eggs, large & preferably pastured

½ tsp. Ginger Powder

½ cup Coconut Milk, unsweetened

Dash of Salt & Pepper

1/3 cup Maple Syrup

½ tsp. Baking Soda

1 tsp. Vanilla Extract

2 tsp. Turmeric

Directions:

Preheat the oven to 350 ° F.

After that, mix eggs, vanilla extract, milk, maple syrup, and milk in a large mixing bowl until combined well.

In another bowl, combine turmeric, coconut flour, ginger powder, baking soda, pepper, and salt.

Now, stir in the coconut flour mixture gradually to the milk mixture until you get a smooth batter.

Then, pour the smooth mixture to paper-lined muffin pan while distributing it evenly.

Finally, bake them for 20 to 25 minutes or until slightly browned at the edges.

Allow the muffins to cool completely.

Tip: They are freezer friendly and stay good for one month.

Nutrition:

Calories: 22Kcal

Proteins:1.1g

Carbohydrates: 2.1g

Fat: 1.2g

Coffee Protein Bars

Preparation Time: 10 Minutes

Cooking Time: 10 Minutes

Servings: 12

Ingredients:

2 cups Nuts

5 tbsp. Water

1 cup Egg White Protein Powder

18 Medjool Dates, large & pitted

¼ cup Cocoa Powder, unsweetened

3 tbsp. Instant Coffee

Directions:

First, blend nuts, instant coffee, egg white protein powder, and cocoa in a food processor until broken down into smaller pieces. Tip: Make sure not to over-process them.

After that, stir in the dates and process them again.

Then, spoon in one tablespoon of water gradually to the processor while it is running or until you get a sticky mixture.

Now, transfer the mixture to a parchment paper-lined baking sheet and spread it across evenly.

Next, place the baking sheet in the refrigerator for 1 hour or until set. Slice them into bars.

Tip: If you prefer, you can add cacao nibs.

Nutrition:

Calories: 196Kcal

Proteins: 11g

Carbohydrates: 23g

Fat: 8g

Cauliflower Popcorn

Preparation Time: 10 Minutes

Cooking Time: 25 Minutes

Servings: 1

Ingredients:

4 cups Cauliflower, broken into florets

Salt, as needed

2 tsp. Extra Virgin Olive Oil

Directions:

First, toss together the cauliflower florets and extra virgin olive oil in a large mixing bowl until coated well.

To this, spoon in the salt and toss well.

Next, bake them for 28 to 30 minutes at 450 °F or until browned and tender.

Serve with more extra olive oil if needed.

Tip: You can even add cayenne pepper to it if you prefer to make it spicy.

Nutrition:

Calories: 90Kcal

Proteins: 4g

Carbohydrates: 10g

Fat: 5g

Spiced Pumpkin Seeds

Preparation Time: 10 Minutes

Cooking Time: 15 Minutes

Servings: Makes 1 cup

Ingredients:

1 cup Pumpkin Seeds

1 tsp. Celtic Sea Salt

2 tsp. Olive Oil

1 tbsp. Chili Powder

Directions:

To start with, keep the pumpkin seeds in a large-sized iron cast skillet over medium-high heat.

Roast them for 3 minutes while stirring it frequently.

After that, take the skillet from the heat and to this, spoon in the chili powder and sea salt. Toss well.

Finally, allow it to cool completely and serve.

Tip: You can reduce or increase the chili powder according to your liking.

Nutrition:

Calories: 106Kcal

Proteins:4.4g

Carbohydrates: 3.6g

Fat: 9.2g

Curry Roasted Chickpeas

Preparation Time: 10 Minutes

Cooking Time: 40 Minutes

Servings: 4

Ingredients:

1 tbsp. Olive Oil

2 tsp. Curry Powder

15 oz. Garbanzo Beans or Chickpeas, washed & drained

½ tsp. Sea Salt

Directions:

First, preheat the oven to 400 ° F.

Next, place the chickpeas, salt, olive oil, and curry powder in a large mixing bowl and combine them well.

Now, transfer the seasoned chickpeas to a baking sheet and spread them in a single layer.

After that, bake them for 25 to 30 minutes or until crispy while turning them once in between.

Allow them to cool completely and serve.

Tip: You can reduce or increase the curry powder according to your spice level.

Nutrition:

Calories: 420Kcal

Proteins: 20.7g

Carbohydrates: 65.1g

Fat: 10.1g

Coconut Oats Balls

Preparation Time: 10 Minutes

Cooking Time: 40 Minutes

Servings: Makes 50

Ingredients:

2/3 cup Honey

2 cups Steel Oats

2 tsp. Vanilla Extract

1 ½ cup Coconut Flakes, unsweetened

1 cup Almonds, chopped

1 cup Peanut Butter

Directions:

For making these energy balls, you first need to place the oats in the food processor and then process them until broken down.

Next, combine the rest of the ingredients in a large mixing bowl until everything comes together.

Now, by using your hands, make balls out of this smooth dough.

Then, place the balls in the refrigerator for half an hour or until set.

Serve and enjoy.

Tip: You can reduce or increase the curry powder according to your spice level.

Nutrition:

Calories: 88Kcal

Proteins:2g

Carbohydrates: 9g

Fat: 5g

Seasoned Coconut Flakes

Preparation Time: 5 Minutes

Cooking Time: 5 Minutes

Servings: 2

Ingredients:

¼ tsp. Nutmeg

1 cup Coconut Flakes, unsweetened

1 tsp. Coconut Oil

1 tsp. Cinnamon

¼ tsp. Salt

¼ tsp. Allspice

Directions:

Preheat the oven to 350 ° F.

After that, place all the ingredients needed to make the savory snacks, excluding the coconut oil in a large zip lock bags. Shake well.

Next, spoon in the coconut oil to the bag and shake again, so the seasoning coats the coconut flakes.

Now, transfer the seasoned coconut to a greased baking sheet.

Then, place the sheet in the middle rack and bake the coconut flakes for 4 to 5 minutes. Tip: Make sure not to over bake them.

Finally, remove the sheet from the oven immediately and allow it to cool completely before serving.

Tip: You can add a low-carb sweetener of your choice to it if desired.

Nutrition:

Calories: 90Kcal

Proteins:1g

Carbohydrates: 4.6g

Fat: 7.8g

Chapter 8. Seafood Recipes

Poached Halibut and Mushrooms

Preparation Time: 5 Minutes

Cooking Time: 30 Minutes

Servings: 8

Ingredients:

2 pounds halibut, cut into bite-sized pieces

1 teaspoon fresh lemon juice

½ teaspoon soy sauce

1/8 teaspoon sesame oil

4 cups mushrooms, sliced

¼ cup water

Salt and pepper to taste

¾ cup green onions

Instructions:

Place a heavy bottomed pot on medium high fire.

Add all ingredients and mix well.

Cover and bring to a boil. Once boiling, lower fire to a simmer. Cook for 25 minutes.

Adjust seasoning to taste.

Serve and enjoy.

Nutrition:

Calories 217, Total Fat 15.8g, Saturated Fat 5.3g, Total Carbs 1.1g, Net Carbs 0.7g, Protein 16.5g, Sugar: 0g, Fiber 0.4g, Sodium 97mg, Potassium 234mg

Halibut Stir Fry

Preparation Time: 5 Minutes

Cooking Time: 20 Minutes

Servings: 6

Ingredients:

2 pounds halibut fillets

2 tbsp olive oil

½ cup fresh parsley

1 onion, sliced

2 stalks celery, chopped

2 tablespoons capers

4 cloves of garlic minced

Salt and pepper to taste

Instructions:

Place a heavy bottomed pot on high fire and heat for 2 minutes. Add oil and heat for 2 more minutes.

Stir in garlic and onions. Sauté for 5 minutes.

Add remaining ingredients, except for parsley and stir fry for 10 minutes or until fish is cooked.

Adjust seasoning to taste and serve with a sprinkle of parsley.

Nutrition:

Calories 331, Total Fat 26g, Saturated Fat 4g, Total Carbs 2g, Net Carbs 1.5g, Protein 22g, Sugar: 0.6g, Fiber 0.5g, Sodium 197mg, Potassium 485mg

Steamed Garlic-Dill Halibut

Preparation Time: 5 Minutes

Cooking Time: 25 Minutes

Servings: 4

Ingredients:

1-pound halibut fillet

1 lemon, freshly squeezed

Salt and pepper to taste

1 teaspoon garlic powder

1 tablespoon dill weed, chopped

Instructions:

Place a large pot on medium fire and fill up to 1.5-inches of water. Place a trivet inside pot.

In a baking dish that fits inside your large pot, add all ingredients and mix well. Cover dish with foil. Place the dish on top of the trivet inside the pot.

Cover pot and steam fish for 15 minutes.

Let fish rest for at least 10 minutes before removing from pot.

Serve and enjoy.

Nutrition:

Calories 270, Total Fat 6.5g, Saturated Fat 0.5g, Total Carbs 3.9g, Net Carbs 1.8g, Protein 47.8g, Sugar: 0g, Fiber 2.1g, Sodium 565mg, Potassium 356mg

Italian Halibut Chowder

Preparation Time: 5 Minutes

Cooking Time: 20 Minutes

Servings: 8

Ingredients:

2 tablespoons olive oil

1 onion, chopped

3 stalks of celery, chopped

3 cloves of garlic, minced

2 ½ pounds halibut steaks, cubed

1 red bell pepper, seeded and chopped

1 cup tomato juice

½ cup apple juice, organic and unsweetened

½ teaspoon dried basil

1/8 teaspoon dried thyme

Salt and pepper to taste

Instructions:

Place a heavy bottomed pot on medium high fire and heat pot for 2 minutes. Add oil and heat for a minute.

Sauté the onion, celery and garlic until fragrant.

Stir in the halibut steaks and bell pepper. Sauté for 3 minutes.

Pour in the rest of the ingredients and mix well.

Cover and bring to a boil. Once boiling, lower fire to a simmer and simmer for 10 minutes.

Adjust seasoning to taste.

Serve and enjoy.

Nutrition:

Calories 318, Total Fat 23g, Saturated Fat 3.9g, Total Carbs 6g, Net Carbs 5g, Protein 21g, Sugar: 4g, Fiber 1g, Sodium 155mg, Potassium 533mg

Pomegranate-Molasses Glazed Salmon

Preparation Time: 15 Minutes

Cooking Time: 20 Minutes

Servings: 4

Ingredients:

1 tbsp coconut oil

2 tbsp pomegranate molasses

¼ cup fresh orange juice

4 garlic cloves, crushed

1 tbsp fresh ginger, grated

4 pcs 8-oz salmon fillets

Instructions:

Mix the garlic, ginger, pomegranate molasses and orange juice in a small bowl.

Pour the mixture over the salmon and marinate at room temperature for 15 minutes.

Preheat the oven to 425 degrees Fahrenheit.

Line a baking sheet with foil and grease it with coconut oil.

Place the salmon skin-side-down on the baking sheet.

Drizzle more pomegranate molasses on top of the salmon.

Bake the fillets for 15 minutes or until the salmon becomes flaky.

Nutrition:

Calories 203, Total Fat 7g, Saturated Fat 3.5g, Total Carbs 29g, Net Carbs 23g, Protein 9g, Sugar: 21g, Fiber 6g, Sodium 128mg, Potassium 472mg

Quick Thai Cod Curry

Preparation Time: 15 Minutes

Cooking Time: 15 Minutes

Servings: 1

Ingredients:

1 tsp coconut oil

1 tablespoon organic Thai red curry paste

1 clove of garlic, minced

1 shallot, minced

1/4 cup coconut cream

3 tbsp water

1 cod fillet

Instructions:

Place a heavy bottomed pot on medium high fire and heat pot for 2 minutes. Add oil and heat for a minute.

Sauté the curry paste, garlic, and shallots until fragrant.

Stir in coconut cream and fillet. Sauté for 3 minutes. Season with pepper and salt to taste.

Cover and bring to a boil. Once boiling, lower fire to a simmer and simmer for 10 minutes.

Adjust seasoning to taste.

Serve and enjoy.

Nutrition:

Calories 458, Total Fat 28g, Saturated Fat 4.8g, Total Carbs 10g, Net Carbs 5g, Protein 45g, Sugar: 1g, Fiber 5g, Sodium 132mg, Potassium 1268mg

Salmon with Sun-Dried Tomatoes and Capers

Preparation Time: 10 Minutes

Cooking Time: 15 Minutes

Servings: 2

Ingredients:

1 salmon fillet

½ lemon, freshly squeezed

Salt and pepper to taste

¼ teaspoon cayenne pepper

½ teaspoon dried oregano

½ teaspoon dried thyme

2 cloves of garlic, minced

2 tablespoons chopped sun-dried tomatoes

1 tablespoon capers

¼ cup water

Instructions:

Place a heavy bottomed pot on medium high fire and add all ingredients.

Mix well, cover and bring to a boil. Once boiling, lower fire to a simmer and simmer for 10 minutes.

Adjust seasoning to taste and continue cooking for another 5 minutes.

Serve and enjoy.

Nutrition:

Calories 265, Total Fat 8g, Saturated Fat 1.7g, Total Carbs 6g, Net Carbs 3g, Protein 41g, Sugar: 3g, Fiber 1g, Sodium 211mg, Potassium 1078g

Island Style Sardines

Preparation Time: 10 Minutes

Cooking Time: 8 hours

Servings: 4

Ingredients:

2 tablespoons olive oil

1 roma tomato, diced

¼ cup sliced onion

1 clove of garlic, minced

1 teaspoon cayenne pepper flakes

½ pound sardines, gutted and scales removed

1 tablespoon lemon juice, freshly squeezed

A dash of rosemary

A dash of sage

Salt and pepper to taste

Instructions:

In a slow cooker, add all ingredients and mix well.

Cover and cook on low settings for 8 hours.

Adjust seasoning if needed.

Serve and enjoy.

Nutrition:

Calories 195, Total Fat 13.5g, Saturated Fat 2g, Total Carbs 4g, Net Carbs 3g, Protein 15g, Sugar: 2g, Fiber 1g, Sodium 177mg, Potassium 366g

Slow Cooked Spanish Cod

Preparation Time: 10 Minutes

Cooking Time: 6 Minutes

Servings: 6

Ingredients:

1 tablespoon olive oil

¼ cup chopped onion

2 tablespoons chopped garlic

1 cup tomato sauce

15 cherry tomatoes, halved

½ cup chopped green olives

Salt and pepper to taste

6 cod fillets, sliced

Instructions:

In a slow cooker, add all ingredients and mix well.

Cover and cook on low settings for 6 hours.

Adjust seasoning if needed.

Serve and enjoy.

Nutrition:

Calories 293, Total Fat 18g, Saturated Fat 3g, Total Carbs 14g, Net Carbs 10g, Protein 21g, Sugar: 4g, Fiber 7g, Sodium 428mg, Potassium 776mg

Multi-Spice Cod Curry

Preparation Time: 15 Minutes

Cooking Time: 20 Minutes

Servings: 6

Ingredients:

2 tablespoons olive oil

1 onion, chopped

1 teaspoon garlic paste

1 teaspoon grated ginger

2 teaspoons cumin

2 teaspoons coriander

1 teaspoon cardamom

½ teaspoon turmeric

Salt and pepper to taste

2 fresh jalapeno peppers, chopped

1 tablespoon lemon juice, freshly squeezed

1 cup tomatoes, diced

1-pound cod fillets, cut into chunks

1 cup water

¼ cup cilantro, chopped

Instructions:

Place a heavy bottomed pot on medium high fire and heat pot for 2 minutes. Add oil and heat for a minute.

Sauté the onion, garlic, and ginger until fragrant.

Stir in the cumin, coriander, cardamom, turmeric, salt, and pepper. Sauté for a minute.

Pour in the rest of the ingredients and mix well.

Cover and bring to a boil. Once boiling, lower fire to a simmer and simmer for 10 minutes.

Adjust seasoning to taste and continue cooking for another 5 minutes.

Serve and enjoy.

Nutrition:

Calories 114, Total Fat 5g, Saturated Fat 0.7g, Total Carbs 5g, Net Carbs 4g, Protein 12g, Sugar: 2g, Fiber 1g, Sodium 234mg, Potassium 332mg

Poached Cod Asian Style

Preparation Time: 10 Minutes

Cooking Time: 15 Minutes

Servings: 4

Ingredients:

1-pound cod, cut into chunks

6 tablespoons water

5 tablespoons soy sauce

1 thumb-size ginger, cut into thin strips

4 cloves of garlic, minced

1 tablespoon sesame oil

¾ teaspoon red pepper flakes

¼ teaspoon Chinese five spice powder

Instructions:

Place a heavy bottomed pot on medium high fire and heat pot for 2 minutes. Add oil and heat for a minute.

Sauté the garlic and ginger until fragrant.

Stir in red pepper flakes and Chinese five spice. Sauté for a minute.

Pour in the rest of the ingredients and toss well.

Cover and bring to a boil. Boil for 2 minutes and then turn off fire and let it sit untouched for 5 minutes.

Serve and enjoy.

Nutrition:

Calories 175, Total Fat 8g, Saturated Fat 1.2g, Total Carbs 7g, Net Carbs 6g, Protein 19g, Sugar: 4g, Fiber 1g, Sodium 646mg, Potassium 365g

Basil-Avocado Baked Salmon

Preparation Time: 10 Minutes

Cooking Time: 15 Minutes

Servings: 4

Ingredients:

1 tbsp coconut oil

4 8oz salmon fillets

1 tbsp lemon zest

1 tsp capers

1 ripe avocado

3 cloves garlic, crushed

½ cup chopped fresh basil

Instructions:

Grease a baking sheet with coconut oil.

On a bowl, mash avocado until it becomes creamy. Add in the chopped garlic, capers, lemon zest and basil. Set aside.

Lay the salmon fillets on the baking sheet and spread the avocado topping on top of the salmon.

Bake in a preheated 350-degree oven for 15 minutes.

Nutrition:

Calories 387, Total Fat 19g, Saturated Fat 3g, Total Carbs 5g, Net Carbs 1.5g, Protein 47g, Sugar: 0.5g, Fiber 3.5g, Sodium 133mg, Potassium 1239mg

Spicy Baked Cod

Preparation Time: 15 Minutes

Cooking Time: 15 Minutes

Servings: 5

Ingredients:

2 tablespoons plain non-fat yogurt

1 teaspoon ginger, grated

2 tablespoon curry powder

1 teaspoon soy sauce

1 teaspoon rice wine vinegar

2 ½ teaspoon cayenne pepper

5 cod fillets

2 tablespoons olive oil

Instructions:

In a shallow dish mix all ingredients except for oil. Let fish sit in marinade for at least an hour.

When ready, lightly grease cookie sheet with oil and preheat oven to 400oF.

Once preheated, place cod filets on prepped cookie sheet and bake to desired doneness, around 15 minutes baking time.

Serve and enjoy.

Nutrition:

Calories 254, Total Fat 8g, Saturated Fat 1g, Total Carbs 2g, Net Carbs 0.4g, Protein 42g, Sugar: 0.5g, Fiber 1.6g, Sodium 144mg, Potassium 1013mg

Cod Casserole Portuguese Style

Preparation Time: 10 Minutes

Cooking Time: 15 Minutes

Servings: 5

Ingredients:

2 tablespoons olive oil

2 cloves of garlic, minced

3 large onion, sliced

2 pounds cod fish, sliced into strips

4 potatoes, peeled and sliced

1 teaspoon paprika

¼ cup tablespoons tomato sauce

¼ cup water

1 ½ teaspoon crushed pepper flakes

1 tablespoon chopped parsley

Instructions:

Place a heavy bottomed pot on medium high fire and heat pot for 2 minutes. Add oil and heat for a minute.

Sauté the garlic and onions until fragrant.

Stir in the cod slices and add the rest of the ingredients.

Season with salt and pepper to taste.

Cover and bring to a boil. Boil for 2 minutes and then lower fire to a simmer. Simmer for 5 minutes. Turn off fire and let it sit untouched for 5 minutes.

Serve and enjoy.

Nutrition:

Calories 337, Total Fat 6g, Saturated Fat 1g, Total Carbs 37g, Net Carbs 31g, Protein 32g, Sugar: 7g, Fiber 6g, Sodium 747mg, Potassium 1246mg

Salmon with Lemon and Dill

Preparation Time: 10 Minutes

Cooking Time: 15 Minutes

Servings: 4

Ingredients:

1-pound salmon fillets

2 tablespoons olive oil

5 tablespoons lemon juice, freshly squeezed

1 tablespoon fresh dill, chopped

¼ teaspoon garlic powder

Salt and pepper to taste

Instructions:

Place a trivet or steamer basket inside your pot and pour water up to an inch high. Bring to a boil.

Place the salmon fillets in a baking dish that will fit in the Pot.

Pour over the rest of the ingredients. Mix well and cover dish securely with foil.

Place the baking dish on the steam rack.

Close the lid and steam fish for 15 minutes. Turn off fire and let fish sit for another 5 minutes.

Serve and enjoy.

Nutrition:

Calories 320, Total Fat 22.1g, Saturated Fat 2.3g, Total Carbs 2.4g, Net Carbs 0.7g, Protein 25.7g, Sugar: 0g, Fiber 1.7g, Sodium 197mg, Potassium 0.3g

Chapter 9. Poultry Recipes

Herbed Chicken Salad

Preparation Time: 15 Minutes

Cooking Time: 10 Minutes

Servings: 4

Ingredients:

6 pitted kalamata olives, halved

1 cup grape tomatoes, halved

1 cup peeled and chopped English cucumbers

8 cups chopped romaine lettuce

1 tsp bottled minced garlic

2 tsp sesame seed paste or tahini

1 cup plain fat-free yogurt

5 tsp fresh lemon juice, divided

1-pound skinless, boneless chicken breast, cut into 1-inch cubes

Cooking spray

½ tsp salt

¾ tsp black pepper, divided

½ tsp garlic powder

1 tsp ground oregano

Instructions:

In a bowl, mix together ¼ tsp salt, ½ tsp pepper, garlic powder and oregano. Then on medium high heat place a skillet and coat with cooking spray and sauté together the spice mixture and chicken until chicken is cooked. Before transferring to bowl, drizzle with juice.

In a small bowl, mix thoroughly the following: garlic, tahini, yogurt, ¼ tsp pepper, ¼ tsp salt, and 2 tsp juice.

In another bowl, mix together olives, tomatoes, cucumber and lettuce.

To Serve salad, place 2 ½ cups of lettuce mixture on plate, topped with ½ cup chicken mixture, 3 tbsp yogurt mixture and 1 tbsp of cheese.

Nutrition:

Calories 291, Total Fat 8g, Saturated Fat 2g, Total Carbs 17g, Net Carbs 14g, Protein 40g, Sugar: 12g, Fiber 3g, Sodium 965mg, Potassium 942mg

Chicken in Pita Bread

Preparation Time: 10 Minutes

Cooking Time: 10 Minutes

Servings: 4

Ingredients:

½ cup diced tomato

2 cups shredded lettuce

4 pcs of 6-inch pitas, cut in half

1 ½ tsp chopped fresh oregano

½ cup plain low-fat yogurt

1 tbsp olive oil

2 tsp grated lemon rind, divided

1 lb. ground chicken

2 large egg whites, lightly beaten

½ tsp coarsely ground black pepper

1 tbsp Greek or Moroccan seasoning blend

½ cup chopped green onions

Instructions:

Mix thoroughly the ground chicken, 1 tsp lemon rind, egg whites, black pepper, Greek or Moroccan seasoning and green onions. Equally separate into eight parts and shaping each part into ¼ inch thick patty.

Turn fire on medium high and place a large nonstick skillet. Fry the patties until browned or for two mins each side. Then slow the fire to medium, cover the skillet and continue cooking for another four minutes.

In a small bowl, mix thoroughly the oregano, yogurt and 1 tsp lemon rind.

To serve, spread the mixture on the pita, add cooked patty, 1 tbsp tomato and ¼ cup lettuce.

Nutrition:

Calories 408, Total Fat 15g, Saturated Fat 4g, Total Carbs 41g, Net Carbs 35g, Protein 30g, Sugar: 4g, Fiber 6g, Sodium 560mg, Potassium 952mg

Greek Chicken Stew

Preparation Time: 10 Minutes

Cooking Time: 40 Minutes

Servings: 8

Ingredients:

1 ½ cups chicken stock or more if needed

2 bay leaves

1 pinch dried oregano or to taste

Salt and ground black pepper to taste

2 tbsp chopped fresh parsley

1 cup tomato sauce

½ cup water

2 cloves garlic, finely chopped

1 pc, 2lbs whole chicken cut into pieces

1 tbsp olive oil

10 small shallots, peeled

Instructions:

Bring to a boil a small pot of lightly salted water. Mix in the shallots and let boil uncovered until tender for around three minutes. Then drain the shallots and dip in cold water until no longer warm.

In another large pot over medium fire, heat olive oil for a minute. Then sauté in the chicken and shallots for 15 minutes or until chicken is cooked and shallots are soft and translucent. Then add the chopped garlic and cook for three mins more.

Then add bay leaves, oregano, salt and pepper, parsley, tomato sauce and the water. Let simmer for a minute before adding the chicken stock. Stir before covering and let cook for 20 minutes on medium-low fire or until chicken is tender.

Nutrition:

Calories 129, Total Fat 3g, Saturated Fat 0.6g, Total Carbs 10g, Net Carbs 7g, Protein 13g, Sugar: 5g, Fiber 3g, Sodium 651mg, Potassium 336mg

Easy Stir-Fried Chicken

Preparation Time: 10 Minutes

Cooking Time: 12 Minutes

Servings: 3

Ingredients:

1 tbsp soy sauce

1 tbsp virgin coconut oil

¼ medium onion, sliced thinly

¼ lb. brown mushrooms

1 large orange bell pepper

2 7-oz skinless and boneless chicken breast

Instructions:

On medium high fire, place a nonstick saucepan and heat coconut oil.

Add soy sauce, onion powder, mushrooms, bell pepper and chicken.

Stir fry for 8 to 10 minutes.

Remove from pan and serve.

Nutrition:

Calories 277, Total Fat 10g, Saturated Fat 2g, Total Carbs 4g, Net Carbs 3g, Protein 44g, Sugar: 2g, Fiber 1g, Sodium 146mg, Potassium 689mg

African Chicken Stew

Preparation Time: 10 Minutes

Cooking Time: 85 Minutes

Servings: 8

Ingredients:

1 lime cut into wedges

2 lbs. bone in, skin on drumsticks and chicken thighs

¼ tsp ground allspice

½ tsp salt

½ tsp pepper

2 bay leaves

1 jalapeno pepper, seeds removed, diced

6 cloves garlic, minced

4 onions, sliced

1 tbsp zest of lemon

¼ cup lemon juice

¼ cup apple cider vinegar

2 tbsp olive oil

¼ cup water

Instructions:

In wide and shallow bowl with lid, combine allspice, salt, pepper, bay leaves, jalapeno, garlic, lemon zest, lemon juice, vinegar and oil. Mix well.

Add chicken, cover and marinate in the ref. Ensuring to turn chicken in two hours. Chicken is best left overnight or for at least 4 hours.

Once you are done marinating, grease a roasting pan and preheat oven to 400oF.

Remove chicken from marinade and arrange on prepared pan. Pop in the oven and bake until juices run clear around 35-40 minutes.

Meanwhile, discard 3/4s of the marinade while reserving onions. Then place a nonstick pan on low fire and add remaining marinade with bay leaves and onions. Sauté for 45 minutes until caramelized while stirring every once in a while.

To serve, place baked chicken on a plate drizzled with caramelized onion sauce and lime wedges on the side.

Also best eaten with plain white rice.

Nutrition:

Calories 543, Total Fat 54g, Saturated Fat 6g, Total Carbs 4g, Net Carbs 3.7g, Protein 11g, Sugar: 1.5g, Fiber 0.3g, Sodium 205mg, Potassium 189mg

Roasted Chicken

Preparation Time: 10 Minutes

Cooking Time: 60 Minutes

Servings: 8

Ingredients:

1 bay leaf

4 tbsp orange peel, chopped coarsely

3 cloves garlic

½ tsp thyme

½ tsp black pepper

½ tbsp. salt

1 whole chicken (3 lbs. preferred

Instructions:

Prepare chicken by placing in room temperature for at least an hour.

With paper towels, pat dry chicken inside and out.

As you begin preparing chicken seasoning, preheat oven to 450oF.

In a small bowl, mix thyme, pepper and salt.

Get 1/3 of the seasoning and wipe inside the chicken. Also place inside of the chicken the bay leaf, citrus peel and garlic.

Tuck the wing tips and tie chicken legs together. Spread remaining seasoning all over and around the chicken. Then place on a roasting pan.

Pop in the oven and bake for 50-60 minutes or until chicken is a golden brown, juices run clear or chicken things or breasts register a 160oF temperature.

Remove from oven and let it sit for 15 minutes more before cutting up and the roasted chicken.

Nutrition:

Calories 270, Total Fat 6g, Saturated Fat 1.6g, Total Carbs 1g, Net Carbs 0.6g, Protein 49g, Sugar: 0g, Fiber 0.4g, Sodium 615mg, Potassium 581mg

Turkey Meatballs

Preparation Time: 10 Minutes

Cooking Time: 25 Minutes

Servings: 4

Ingredients:

1 tsp oil

Pepper and salt to taste

1 tsp dried parsley

4 tbsp fresh basil, finely chopped

¼ yellow onion, finely diced

1 14-oz can of artichoke hearts, diced

1 lb. ground turkey

Instructions:

Grease a cookie sheet and preheat oven to 350oF.

On medium fire, place a nonstick medium saucepan and sauté artichoke hearts and diced onions for 5 minutes or until onions are soft.

Remove from fire and let cool.

Meanwhile, in a big bowl, mix with hands parsley, basil and ground turkey. Season to taste.

Once onion mixture has cooled add into the bowl and mix thoroughly.

With an ice cream scooper, scoop ground turkey and form into balls, makes around 6 balls.

Place on prepped cookie sheet, pop in the oven and bake until cooked through around 15-20 minutes.

Remove from pan, serve and enjoy.

Nutrition:

Calories 306, Total Fat 14g, Saturated Fat 3.6g, Total Carbs 12g, Net Carbs 6g, Protein 34g, Sugar: 2g, Fiber 6g, Sodium 197mg, Potassium 770mg

Chicken Breasts with Stuffing

Preparation Time: 10 Minutes

Cooking Time: 40 Minutes

Servings: 8

Ingredients:

8 pcs of 6-oz boneless and skinless chicken breasts

1 tbsp minced fresh basil

2 tbsp finely chopped, pitted Kalamata olives

¼ cup crumbled feta cheese

1 large bell pepper, halved and seeded

Instructions:

In a greased baking sheet place bell pepper with skin facing up and pop into a preheated broiler on high. Broil until blackened around 15 minutes. Remove from broiler and place right away into a re-sealable bag, seal and leave for 15 minutes.

After, peel bell pepper and mince. Preheat grill to medium high fire.

In a medium bowl, mix well basil, olives, cheese and bell pepper.

Form a pocket on each chicken breast by creating a slit through the thickest portion; add 2 tbsp bell pepper mixture and seal with a wooden pick. (At this point, you can stop and freeze chicken and just thaw when needed for grilling already

Season chicken breasts with pepper and salt.

Grill for six minutes per side, remove from grill and cover loosely with foil and let stand for 10 minutes before.

Nutrition:

Calories 221, Total Fat 6g, Saturated Fat 1.7g, Total Carbs 1g, Net Carbs 0.8g, Protein 39g, Sugar: 0.5g, Fiber 0.2g, Sodium 135mg, Potassium 591mg

Chicken-Bell Pepper Sauté

Preparation Time: 10 Minutes

Cooking Time: 30 Minutes

Servings: 6

Ingredients:

6 4-oz skinless, boneless chicken breast halves, cut in half horizontally

Cooking spray

20 Kalamata olives

1 tsp chopped fresh oregano

2 tbsp finely chopped fresh flat-leaf parsley

¼ tsp freshly ground black pepper

½ tsp salt

2 1/3 cups coarsely chopped tomato

1 large red bell pepper, cut into ¼-inch strips

1 large yellow bell pepper, cut into ¼-inch strips

3 cups onion sliced crosswise

1 tbsp olive oil

Instructions:

On medium high fire, place a large nonstick fry pan and heat oil. Once oil is hot, sauté onions until soft and translucent, around 6 to 8 minutes.

Add bell peppers and sauté for another 10 minutes or until tender.

Add black pepper, salt and tomato. Cook until tomato juice has evaporated, around 7 minutes.

Add olives, oregano and parsley, cook until heated through around 1 to 2 minutes. Transfer to a bowl and keep warm.

Wipe pan with paper towel and grease with cooking spray. Return to fire and place chicken breasts. Cook for three minutes per side or until desired doneness is reached. If needed, cook chicken in batches.

When cooking the last batch of chicken is done, add back the previous batch of chicken and the onion-bell pepper mixture and cook for a minute or two while tossing chicken to coat well in the onion-bell pepper mixture.

Serve and enjoy.

Nutrition:

Calories 81, Total Fat 3g, Saturated Fat 0.4g, Total Carbs 4g, Net Carbs 3g, Protein 10g, Sugar: 1.7g, Fiber 1g, Sodium 148mg, Potassium 266mg

Avocado-Orange Grilled Chicken

Preparation Time: 10 Minutes

Cooking Time: 12 Minutes

Servings: 4

Ingredients:

1 small red onion, sliced thinly

2 oranges, peeled and sectioned

¼ cup fresh lime juice

1 avocado

4 pieces of 4-6oz boneless, skinless chicken breasts

Pepper and salt to taste

1 tbsp honey

2 tbsp chopped cilantro

¼ cup minced red onion

1 cup low fat yogurt

Instructions:

In a large bowl mix honey, cilantro, minced red onion and yogurt.

Submerge chicken into mixture and marinate for at least 30 minutes.

Grease grate and preheat grill to medium high fire.

Remove chicken from marinade and season with pepper and salt.

Grill for 6 minutes per side or until chicken is cooked and juices run clear.

Meanwhile, peel avocado and discard seed. Chop avocados and place in bowl. Quickly add lime juice and toss avocado to coat well with juice.

Add cilantro, thinly sliced onions and oranges into bowl of avocado, mix well.

Serve grilled chicken and avocado dressing on the side.

Nutrition:

Calories 443, Total Fat 14g, Saturated Fat 3g, Total Carbs 26g, Net Carbs 20g, Protein 53g, Sugar: 17g, Fiber 6g, Sodium 815mg, Potassium 1039mg

Honey Chicken Tagine

Preparation Time: 10 Minutes

Cooking Time: 1 hour and 20 Minutes

Servings: 12

Ingredients:

1 ½ tbsp honey

1 15-oz can chickpeas, rinsed

12-oz kumquats, seeded and roughly chopped

1 14-oz can vegetable broth

1/8 tsp ground cloves

½ tsp ground pepper

½ tsp salt

¾ tsp ground cinnamon

1 tsp ground cumin

1 tsp ground coriander

2 lbs. boneless, skinless chicken thighs, trimmed of fat and cut into 2-inch pieces

1 tbsp minced fresh ginger

4 cloves garlic, slivered

2 onions, thinly sliced

1 tbsp extra virgin olive oil

Instructions:

Preheat oven to 3750F.

On medium fire, place a heatproof casserole and heat oil.

Add onions and sauté for 4 minutes or until soft.

Add ginger and garlic, sauté for another minute.

Add chicken and sauté for 8 minutes.

Season with cloves, pepper, salt, cinnamon, cumin, and coriander. Sauté for a minute or until aromatic.

Add honey, chickpeas, kumquats, and broth. Bring to a boil and turn off fire.

Cover casserole and pop in the oven. Bake for an hour while stirring every after 15-minute intervals.

Nutrition:

Calories 541, Total Fat 46g, Saturated Fat 6g, Total Carbs 16g, Net Carbs 10g, Protein 20g, Sugar: 6g, Fiber 4g, Sodium 521mg, Potassium 265mg

Brussels Sprouts and Paprika Chicken Thighs

Preparation Time: 10 Minutes

Cooking Time: 25 Minutes

Servings: 4

Ingredients:

4 large bone-in chicken thighs, skin removed

1 tsp dried thyme

1 tbsp smoked paprika

2 cloves garlic, minced

½ tsp ground pepper, divided

¾ tsp salt, divided

3 tbsp extra virgin olive oil, divided

1 lemon, sliced

4 small shallots, quartered

1 lb. Brussels sprouts, trimmed and halved

Instructions:

Preheat oven to 4500F and position rack to lower third in oven.

On a large and rimmed baking sheet, mix ¼ tsp pepper, ¼ tsp salt, 2 tbsp oil, lemon, shallots, and Brussels sprouts.

With a chef's knife, mash ½ tsp salt and garlic to form a paste.

In small bowl, mix ¼ tsp pepper, 1 tbsp oil, thyme, paprika, and garlic paste. Rub all over chicken and place around Brussels sprouts in pan.

Pop in the oven and roast for 20 to 25 minutes or until chicken is cooked and juices run clear.

Serve and enjoy.

Nutrition:

Calories 293, Total Fat 14g, Saturated Fat 3.2g, Total Carbs 15g, Net Carbs 10g, Protein 29g, Sugar: 4g, Fiber 5g, Sodium 992mg, Potassium 769mg

Chapter 10. Vegan and Vegetable Recipes

Nutty and Fruity Garden Salad

Preparation time: 10 minutes

Cooking time: 0 minutes

Servings: 2

Ingredients:

6 cups baby spinach

½ cup chopped walnuts, toasted

1 ripe red pear, sliced

1 ripe persimmon, sliced

1 teaspoon garlic minced

1 shallot, minced

1 tablespoon extra-virgin olive oil

2 tablespoons fresh lemon juice

1 teaspoon whole grain mustard

Instructions:

Mix well garlic, shallot, oil, lemon juice and mustard in a large salad bowl.

Add spinach, pear and persimmon. Toss to coat well.

To serve, garnish with chopped pecans.

Nutrition:

Calories 332, Total Fat 21g, Saturated Fat 2g, Total Carbs 37g, Net Carbs 28g, Protein 7g, Sugar: 20g, Fiber 9g, Sodium 75mg, Potassium 864mg

Creamy Cauliflower-Broccoli Soup

Preparation time: 15 minutes

Cooking time: 15 minutes

Servings: 6

Ingredients:

Pepper and salt to taste

4 cups chicken broth

1 teaspoon dried basil

1 teaspoon dried oregano

½ cup onion, roughly chopped

2 cups carrots, cubed

3 cups cauliflower florets

2 cups broccoli florets

Instructions:

In a large soup pot, bring to a boil chicken broth, basil, oregano and onions. Once boiling, lower fire to a simmer.

Meanwhile, dice cauliflower and broccoli florets. And add to pot. Add carrots, cover and simmer for 10 minutes. Season with pepper and salt to taste.

Turn off fire and allow soup to cool.

Place veggies into a blender while ensuring that liquid is reserved. Puree veggies along with 1 cup of reserved liquid. If you want a thick soup, then 1 cup liquid is enough. If you desire a less thick soup, add more reserved liquid until desired consistency is reached.

Return pureed soup to empty pot and simmer until heated through. Adjust seasoning if needed before serving.

Nutrition:

Calories 39, Total Fat 0.3g, Saturated Fat 0.1g, Total Carbs 8g, Net Carbs 5g, Protein 2g, Sugar: 4g, Fiber 3g, Sodium 47mg, Potassium 348mg

Nutty and Fruity Amaranth Porridge

Preparation time: 10 minutes

Cooking time: 30 minutes

Servings: 2

Ingredients:

1 medium pear, chopped

½ cup blueberries

1 tsp cinnamon

1 tbsp raw honey

¼ cup pumpkin seeds

2 cups filtered water

2/3 cups whole-grain amaranth

Instructions:

In a nonstick pan with cover, boil water and amaranth. Slow fire to a simmer and continue cooking until liquid is absorbed completely, around 25-30 minutes.

Turn off fire.

Mix in cinnamon, honey and pumpkin seeds. Mix well.

Pour equally into two bowls.

Garnish with pear and blueberries.

Serve and enjoy.

Nutrition:

Calories 416, Total Fat 12g, Saturated Fat 2g, Total Carbs 68g, Net Carbs 61g, Protein 14g, Sugar: 23g, Fiber 7g, Sodium 48mg, Potassium 481mg

Korean Barbecue Tofu

Preparation time: 10 minutes

Cooking time: 15 minutes

Servings: 3

Ingredients:

1 tbsp olive oil

2 tsp onion powder

4 garlic cloves, minced

2 tsp dry mustard

3 tbsp brown sugar

½ cup soy sauce

1 ½ lbs. firm tofu, sliced to ¼-inch cubes

Instructions:

In a re-sealable bag, mix all ingredients except for tofu and oil. Mix well until sugar is dissolved.

Add sliced tofu and slowly turn bag to mmix. Seal bag and place flatly inside the ref for an hour.

After an hour, turn bag to the other side and marinate for another hour.

To cook, in a nonstick fry pan, heat oil on medium high fire. Add tofu and stir fry until sides are browned.

Serve and enjoy.

Nutrition:

Calories 437, Total Fat 25g, Saturated Fat 3g, Total Carbs 23g, Net Carbs 15g, Protein 40g, Sugar: 8g, Fiber 6g, Sodium 1600mg, Potassium 724mg

Fruit Bowl with Yogurt Topping

Preparation time: 15 minutes

Cooking time: 0 minutes

Servings: 6

Ingredients:

¼ cup golden brown sugar

2/3 cup minced fresh ginger

1 16-oz Greek yogurt

¼ tsp ground cinnamon

2 tbsp honey

½ cup dried cranberries

3 navel oranges

2 large tangerines

1 pink grapefruit, peeled

Instructions:

Into sections, break tangerines and grapefruit.

Slice tangerine sections in half and grapefruit sections into thirds. Place all sliced fruits and its juices in a large bowl.

Peel oranges, remove pith, slice into ¼-inch thick rounds and then cut into quarters. Transfer to bowl of fruit along with juices.

In bowl, add cinnamon, honey and ¼ cup of cranberries. Place in the ref for an hour.

In a medium bowl mix ginger and yogurt. Place on top of fruit bowl, drizzle with remaining cranberries and brown sugar.

Serve and enjoy.

Nutrition:

Calories 171, Total Fat 1g, Saturated Fat 0.1g, Total Carbs 35g, Net Carbs 32g, Protein 9g, Sugar: 28g, Fiber 3g, Sodium 31mg, Potassium 400mg

Mushroom, Spinach and Turmeric Frittata

Preparation time: 10 minutes

Cooking time: 40 minutes

Servings: 6

Ingredients:

½ tsp pepper

½ tsp salt

1 tsp turmeric

5-oz firm tofu

4 large eggs

6 large egg whites

¼ cup water

1 lb. fresh spinach

6 cloves freshly chopped garlic

1 large onion, chopped

1 lb. button mushrooms, sliced

Instructions:

Grease a 10-inch nonstick and oven proof skillet and preheat oven to 350oF.

Place skillet on medium high fire and add mushrooms. Cook until golden brown.

Add onions, cook for 3 minutes or until onions are tender.

Add garlic, sauté for 30 seconds.

Add water and spinach, cook while covered until spinach is wilted, around 2 minutes.

Remove lid and continue cooking until water is fully evaporated.

In a blender, puree pepper, salt, turmeric, tofu, eggs and egg whites until smooth. Pour into skillet once liquid is fully evaporated.

Pop skillet into oven and bake until the center is set around 25-30 minutes.

Remove skillet from oven and let it stand for ten minutes before inverting and transferring to a serving plate.

Cut into 6 equal wedges, serve and enjoy.

Nutrition:

Calories 358, Total Fat 6g, Saturated Fat 1.6g, Total Carbs 65g, Net Carbs 52g, Protein 21g, Sugar: 4g, Fiber 12g, Sodium 371mg, Potassium 1809mg

Roasted Root Vegetables

Preparation time: 10 minutes

Cooking time: 1 hour and 30 minutes

Servings: 6

Ingredients:

2 tbsp olive oil

1 head garlic, cloves separated and peeled

1 large turnip, peeled and cut into ½-inch pieces

1 medium sized red onion, cut into ½-inch pieces

1 ½ lbs. beets, trimmed but not peeled, scrubbed and cut into ½-inch pieces

1 ½ lbs. Yukon gold potatoes, unpeeled, cut into ½-inch pieces

2 ½ lbs. butternut squash, peeled, seeded, cut into ½-inch pieces

Instructions:

Grease 2 rimmed and large baking sheets. Preheat oven to 425oF.

In a large bowl, mix all ingredients thoroughly.

Into the two baking sheets, evenly divide the root vegetables, spread in one layer.

Season generously with pepper and salt.

Pop into the oven and roast for 1 hour and 15 minute or until golden brown and tender.

Remove from oven and let it cool for at least 15 minutes before serving.

Nutrition:

Calories 278, Total Fat 5g, Saturated Fat 1g, Total Carbs 57g, Net Carbs 47g, Protein 6g, Sugar: 15g, Fiber 10g, Sodium 124mg, Potassium 1598mg

Tropical Fruit Parfait

Preparation time: 10 minutes

Cooking time: 10 minutes

Servings: 1

Ingredients:

1 tbsp toasted sliced almonds

¼ cup plain soy yogurt

½ cup of fruit combination cut into ½-inch cubes (pineapple, mango and kiwi)

Instructions:

Prepare fresh fruit by peeling and slicing into ½-inch cubes.

Place cubed fruit in a bowl and top with a dollop of soy yogurt.

Garnish with sliced almonds and if desired, refrigerate for an hour before serving.

Nutrition:

Calories 119, Total Fat 2g, Saturated Fat 0.1g, Total Carbs 25g, Net Carbs 24g, Protein 2g, Sugar: 21g, Fiber 1g, Sodium 9mg, Potassium 161mg

Cinnamon Chips with Avocado-Strawberry Salsa

Preparation time: 10 minutes

Cooking time: 10 minutes

Servings: 6

Ingredients:

3/8 tsp salt

2 tsp fresh lime juice

1 tsp minced seeded jalapeno pepper

2 tbsp minced fresh cilantro

1 cup finely chopped strawberries

1 ½ cups finely chopped, peeled and ripe avocado

½ tsp ground cinnamon

2 tsp sugar

6 6-inch brown rice tortillas

2 tsp olive oil

Instructions:

Preheat oven to 350oF.

Prepare the cinnamon chips by brushing olive oil all over the brown rice tortilla.

In a small bowl, mix together cinnamon and sugar.

Sprinkle cinnamon-sugar mixture evenly all over each of the brown rice tortilla.

Cut up each tortilla into 12 wedges, evenly and place on a baking sheet. If needed you can bake tortilla in two batches.

Pop the tortillas into the oven and bake until crisped, around 10 minutes. Remove from oven and keep warm.

Meanwhile, prepare salsa by mixing the remaining ingredients in a medium bowl. Stir to mix well.

To enjoy, dip crisped tortillas into bowl of salsa and eat or, you can spread the fruity salsa all over one tortilla chip and enjoy.

Nutrition:

Calories 213, Total Fat 11g, Saturated Fat 3g, Total Carbs 25g, Net Carbs 18g, Protein 5g, Sugar: 4g, Fiber 7g, Sodium 362mg, Potassium 337mg

Stir Fried Brussels Sprouts and Carrots

Preparation time: 10 minutes

Cooking time: 15 minutes

Servings: 6

Ingredients:

1 tbsp cider vinegar

1/3 cup water

1 lb. Brussels sprouts, halved lengthwise

1 lb. carrots cut diagonally into ½-inch thick lengths

3 tbsp olive oil, divided

2 tbsp chopped shallot

½ tsp pepper

¾ tsp salt

Instructions:

On medium high fire, place a nonstick medium fry pan and heat 2 tbsp oil.

Ass shallots and cook until softened, around one to two minutes while occasionally stirring.

Add pepper salt, Brussels sprouts and carrots. Stir fry until vegetables starts to brown on the edges, around 3 to 4 minutes.

Add water, cook and cover.

After 5 to 8 minutes, or when veggies are already soft, add remaining butter.

If needed season with more pepper and salt to taste.

Turn off fire, transfer to a platter, serve and enjoy.

Nutrition:

Calories 98, Total Fat 4g, Saturated Fat 2g, Total Carbs 14g, Net Carbs 9g, Protein 3g, Sugar: 5g, Fiber 5g, Sodium 357mg, Potassium 502mg

Curried Veggies and Poached Eggs

Preparation time: 10 minutes

Cooking time: 50 minutes

Servings: 4

Ingredients:

4 large eggs

½ tsp white vinegar

1/8 tsp crushed red pepper – optional

1 cup water

1 14-oz can chickpeas, drained

2 medium zucchinis, diced

½ lb. sliced button mushrooms

1 tbsp yellow curry powder

2 cloves garlic, minced

1 large onion, chopped

2 tsp extra virgin olive oil

Instructions:

On medium high fire, place a large saucepan and heat oil.

Sauté onions until tender around four to five minutes.

Add garlic and continue sautéing for another half minute.

Add curry powder, stir and cook until fragrant around one to two minutes.

Add mushrooms, mix, cover and cook for 5 to 8 minutes or until mushrooms are tender and have released their liquid.

Add red pepper if using, water, chickpeas and zucchini. Mix well to combine and bring to a boil.

Once boiling, reduce fire to a simmer, cover and cook until zucchini is tender around 15 to 20 minutes of simmering.

Meanwhile, in a small pot filled with 3-inches deep of water, bring to a boil on high fire.

Once boiling, reduce fire to a simmer and add vinegar.

Slowly add one egg, slipping it gently into the water. Allow to simmer until egg is cooked, around 3 to 5 minutes.

Remove egg with a slotted spoon and transfer to a plate, one plate one egg.

Repeat the process with remaining eggs.

Once the veggies are done cooking, divide evenly into 4 servings and place one serving per plate of egg.

Serve and enjoy.

Nutrition:

Calories 254, Total Fat 9g, Saturated Fat 2g, Total Carbs 30g, Net Carbs 21g, Protein 16g, Sugar: 7g, Fiber 9g, Sodium 341mg, Potassium 480mg

Conclusion

The anti-inflammatory diet is a perfect solution to enjoy mouth-watering foods at home every day. Recipes prepared by following the basic principles of this diet not only take care of your health but also your cravings to enjoy delicious meals. Also, they can significantly assist in keeping your weight under check.

This book aims to educate its readers about the benefits of the anti-inflammatory diet and to inspire switching to a healthy lifestyle without compromising on taste. A great variety of healthy recipes is provided in the book, which you can prepare at home anytime you want and enjoy them guilt-free.

Changing your lifestyle to include a healthier way of eating is not easy, though it can be done. For many people, the prospect of going on a diet is a temporary fix that they expect will result in a long-term result, which is never the case. In order to stick with a healthy diet, it's important to maintain focus, keep a positive outlook, and join support groups, whether it's online or in-person, or both. If you find yourself getting discouraged, just remember that this momentary and staying on track for the sake of improving your health is most important.

Here are a few tips and suggestions to keep in mind while making important changes to your diet and lifestyle:

•   Try new foods and don't be afraid to taste something that's different, unique, or even unusual. Many exotic fruits and vegetables offer distinctive tastes, as well as health benefits that we may not be aware of. Mangos, guava, jackfruit, and seaweed are among some common and delicious options to try. Even some everyday foods that we pass by in the grocery store, such as avocado, aloe, lentils, and other foods that are nutritious and useful can be easily added to our everyday routine.

- Try a new recipe at least once a week, or if you're busy, once every two weeks. It doesn't have to be a complex option to impress guests, but merely a simple 3-4 ingredient dish that you enjoy. It will expand your palette and taste for new meals.

- Stay active and exercise often. Eating well is just one way to combat inflammation. Moving regularly and getting into a routine of exercise is beneficial. Studies indicate a positive impact on weight loss and health improvement from minimal exercise for 30 minutes each session for just three times a week. Walking regularly, cycling, and trying a variety of stretching and strength training exercises can help you develop muscle and tone while improving your health with diet.

- If you suffer from chronic conditions that trigger inflammation, do as much as possible to read and educate yourself on the symptoms, treatments, and what you can do to reduce the effects. Some conditions are difficult to cure, though many of the negative side effects and pain can be greatly reduced by improving diet, exercise, and everyday habits.

- If you smoke or drink excessive alcohol, it's in your best interest to quit both, or at least reduce your drinking significantly while reducing smoking. Since both habits can be difficult to tackle, there are resources available online to curb your cravings, and eating well is one way to improve your body's condition in the meantime.

If you feel discouraged after a while and experience an increase in symptoms associated with inflammation, it's best to check in with your doctor or a specialist to monitor your health and any related condition(s). Continue to eat healthily, and if you "cheat" now and again, just start again. Everyone makes mistakes and changing dietary habits can be challenging for anyone. Sometimes, there are experiences or circumstances in life that cause us to abandon our dietary plans, and this can make returning to this diet, as with any other way of eating, challenging. Always look forward and consider the benefits of following the diet previously, which can be inspiring to begin again.

Printed in Great Britain
by Amazon